THE ECLOGUES AND
THE GEORGICS

VIRGIL

THE ECLOGUES AND THE GEORGICS

TRANSLATED INTO ENGLISH VERSE

BY

R. C. TREVELYAN

CAMBRIDGE
AT THE UNIVERSITY PRESS
1944

CAMBRIDGE
UNIVERSITY PRESS

University Printing House, Cambridge CB2 8BS, United Kingdom

Cambridge University Press is part of the University of Cambridge.

It furthers the University's mission by disseminating knowledge in the pursuit of
education, learning and research at the highest international levels of excellence.

www.cambridge.org
Information on this title: www.cambridge.org/9781107445789

© Cambridge University Press 1944

First published 1944
First paperback edition 2014

A catalogue record for this publication is available from the British Library

ISBN 978-1-107-44578-9 Paperback

To

URSULA WOOD

Within the cool depths of a beech-tree's shade,
Long ago in my boyhood there I found
Tityrus piping on his rustic reed
Sweet woodland melodies. Long and long I listened
Entranced; until he changed his tune and sang
Of flocks and herds, the fruit-tree and the vine,
Of ploughmen and of thrifty bees. And now,
Presumptuously daring, this hard task
Have I essayed, labouring to transplant
These tender flowers of delicate Latin speech
Into an alien soil. My task is ended.
But whom shall it please? Who in this restless age,
So ignorant of its own ignorance,
Has need of the shy beauty and stateliness
Of Virgil's Muse? Few surely.
To most must it not seem
A mere pedantic labour of fond love,
A luxury, outmoded and unwanted?
*   And then I think of you, my friend, remembering*
How for my toil you gave me hope and courage,
Divining through the dim veil of my verses
That antique Roman charm and grandeur, half-revealed,
Which else to you were silent, unenjoyed.
For you too are a servant of the Muses:
Their garden is your heritage, but therein
You are their labourer, with no reward
Save freedom there to plant and rear new flowers and fruits
For our delight and wonder, or to engraft
Upon old stems new shoots.
*   But whence the spirit of enchantment blows,*

What matter, so it but inspire the mind
Of one fit to receive that sudden glory,
And give it form and feature?
Or rather of itself each winged thought
Glides swift as light through dull familiar words,
Kindling and weaving them till they become
A garment for its beauty and its power.
Happy then must those be, who in youth's prime
Have sought and won that mastery of words
By which alone the breath of poetry
In all its infinite delicacies and pride
May be clothed and revealed. Great is the word;
Yet is the spirit greater. For if its breath
Blows not, like a fading coal the word
Fades and is dead. Then let the house be swept
And garnished at all hours
Against the arrival of its sovereign lord,
The bride-groom of the mind, who unannounced
In his own time shall come; whom we must watch
And wait for night and day; and when he comes
Must spend our toil to entertain him royally.
   With his whole soul and strength
Did Virgil labour: so must we. With naught
Less than perfection might he rest content.
So, when he lay dying,
From time to time he asked his friends to bring him
The book-boxes wherein his Aeneid lay—
With all its blemishes and incompletions,
Its ambiguities and sublime defects—
That he might burn it: but they shook their heads
Weeping, though he besought them earnestly.
Thus, like a lover still unsatisfied,
Heart-broken, did death take him; but his book,
That so long he had loved and laboured for,
Death has no power to touch.

CONTENTS

PART I   THE ECLOGUES

Introduction   *page* 1

ECLOGUE I.   Tityrus   5

II.   Alexis   8

III.   Palaemon   10

IV.   Pollio   14

V.   Daphnis   16

VI.   Varus   19

VII.   Meliboeus   22

VIII.   Pharmaceutria   24

IX.   Moeris   28

X.   Gallus   31

PART II   THE GEORGICS

Introduction   35

BOOK I   38

II   57

III   77

IV   98

PART I   THE ECLOGUES

INTRODUCTION

These ten short poems, called *Bucolics* or *Eclogues*, which are the earliest works that can be certainly attributed to Virgil, were probably written between 41 B.C. and 37 B.C.

Virgil's unassailable fame as one of the greatest of poets does not rest upon his *Eclogues*, but upon his *Georgics* and *Aeneid*; yet it has been the fate of these immature experiments to have had a greater influence upon European literature than almost any other poems. It was they, rather than their parent Theocritus, that became the fountain-head of the vast stream of Renaissance pastoral writers, Italian, Spanish, French and English. Tasso and Ronsard, Spenser, Sydney and Milton, and the innumerable flock of lesser pastoralists, have all been inspired by and borrowed from them; and their spirit, though not their form, may still be discovered in *Adonais* and *Thyrsis*—and also in that last pathetic madness of Don Quixote, when he resolved to live the life of an ideal shepherd, 'and entertain himself among the deserts and solitary places of that country, where he might freely vent out and give scope unto his amorous passions by exercising himself in commendable and virtuous pastoral exercises'.

In one of his letters from India Macaulay made the confession that Virgil, whom he had been re-reading, had not the power to charm him so much as he used to do. He goes on to say: 'The *Georgics* pleased me better; the *Eclogues* best—the second and tenth above all.' Few lovers of Virgil are likely to agree with this verdict; yet it is no more preposterous than the preference that is so often felt by the common reader for Milton's early poems over his later poems. The *Eclogues* are indeed even more artificial and imitative than *Lycidas*, and few of them are such perfect works of art as *L'Allegro* and *Il Penseroso*, or *Comus*. But conventional and unreal as their pseudo-pastoral themes may be, the texture and phrasing of the verse is almost always exquisite and delightful. They, even more than the *Georgics*, are pure poetry, by which I mean poetry whose power to charm consists almost entirely in the physical beauty of the verse, its imagery, and the atmosphere or the sentiment which it expresses. They are seldom what we can call 'great poetry'; though it would seem unreasonable to refuse that description to such lines as the last two of the first Eclogue:

> *Et jam summa procul villarum culmina fumant,*
> *Majoresque cadunt altis de montibus umbrae—*

or as this passage from Eclogue v:

> *Nam neque me tantum venientis sibilus Austri*
> *Nec percussa juvant fluctu tam litora, nec quae*
> *Saxosas inter decurrunt flumina valles—*

lines which, though reminiscent of Theocritus, are no imitations, but are purely Virgilian in quality and sentiment.

It is true that many passages in the *Eclogues* are echoes, sometimes almost literal translations of Theocritus; but it is wiser to forget Theocritus (as Virgil doubtless intended his readers to do) and to enjoy the poetry as it deserves to be enjoyed. Sometimes however, as in the second half of the sixth Eclogue, the Greek poem that he is imitating is so immeasurably superior in its passion and realism and romantic beauty, that the Latin poem seems to be no better than a frigid and uninspired copy. It must be admitted that in these youthful poems Virgil was far inferior to Theocritus in dramatic sense, and in the power of suggesting real human beings. The language talked by his shadowy Mantuan-Sicilian-Arcadian shepherds and goatherds is not racy of any particular Italian soil, but is very much the same as the elaborate poetic diction of the *Georgics* or the *Aeneid*.

Moreover the scenery varies in character even within the same poem. Sometimes it is the Mincius, flowing lazily between gently sloping hills and beech-groves (but there are neither hills nor beeches near Mantua); sometimes the green-clothed crags and caves, and the steep mountains of Sicily and southern Italy. But this eclectic fairyland and its idyllic inhabitants should be no more difficult for the imagination to accept than the Elizabethan Attica of the *Midsummer Night's Dream*, or the sea-coasts of Bohemia.

A more serious stumbling-block for modern readers is the introduction of the poet himself in pastoral disguise, as Tityrus the farm-servant, and

Menalcas, the shepherd poet, and the appearance of his patron, the poet and general Gallus, as a bucolic hero, dying for love of the actress Cytheris. The sixth and eighth Eclogues are disfigured by flatteries of Varus; though Virgil's compliments to Octavian in the first Eclogue are no doubt the expression of genuine gratitude and admiration. Such incongruities, though confusing and regrettable, do no very serious damage to the beauty of the poems, and should amuse rather than disgust.

It is always interesting to compare the early experiments of a great artist with his mature works. In the *Bucolics* Virgil already shows himself a deliberate and fastidious craftsman; and his mastery of phrasing and of metre is sufficient for what we might call his Theocritean Muse, who demands no sustained movement, no 'linkèd sweetness long drawn out', but is content with short periods and end-stopped lines. There is little promise of the intricate and subtle versification which is to be the glory of the *Aeneid*. Again, neither in these poems nor in the *Georgics* do we find his later stylistic habit, so omnipresent in the *Aeneid*, of 'theme and variation', of which the following lines furnish two examples:

> *Trojanas ut opes et lamentabile regnum*
> *Eruerint Danai, quaeque ipse miserrima vidi,*
> *Et quorum pars magna fui.*   (*Aeneid* II, 4.)

Of such devices Virgil has no need for his present homelier purposes. As yet he rarely attempts the sublime; and when he does, as in the fourth Eclogue, the lines, though dignified and impressive, have none of the freedom and variety of movement which we find, for instance, in the marvellous finale of the sixth Aeneid.

The metre, which I have used, is an unrimed verse of seven, and occasionally eight, accents. Its structure is the same as that of the normal half-stanza of the English ballad, such as:

> And mony was the feather bed
> That flattered on the faem.

I have found that a close translation of a hexameter proves, on the average, to be about the same length as this English verse, and so have been able to translate line for line with very little omission or expansion. The hexameter is undoubtedly a more beautiful and varied medium; but the English metre has at least the merit of swiftness of movement, and can be given considerable variety by frequently changing the place of the caesura, which normally follows the fourth accent. Sometimes I have omitted the syllable that should carry the fourth accent, as in the last line of the first Eclogue:

And longer fall the shadows from the high mountain crests.

Sometimes, again, I have added two extra syllables at the end of the line, as in the first line of the first Eclogue:

Tityrus, thou reclined beneath the covert of a spreading beech.

These are easy and natural variations of the metre, because in a line of seven or eight accents there is a tendency for the first, third, fifth and seventh stresses to be slightly more prominent than the second, fourth, sixth and eighth, so that if the weak fourth stress be dropped, or an eighth stress added, the fundamental rhythm is not impaired. This alternation of stronger and weaker accents causes a kind of undulation in the rhythm, which gives lightness and swiftness to the verse.

ECLOGUE I

TITYRUS

After the defeat of Brutus and Cassius, the Triumvirs assigned to their
veterans the lands of various Italian cities. Virgil's father was thus
threatened with ejection from his farm near Mantua, whereupon Virgil
went to Rome, and there, in a personal interview with Caesar Octavius,
obtained restitution of his father's land.

Such is the background of this Eclogue, in which the shepherd Meliboeus,
who has been expelled from his homestead, meets with Tityrus, a more
fortunate shepherd, who has lately gone to Rome in order to buy his
freedom. But, as T. E. Page remarks in his commentary, the elderly
farm-slave Tityrus, who obtains his freedom from his master, disappears
and makes room for the young Virgil, who recovers his father's farm by
the grace of Octavius. 'The transformation is made with such delicate
skill that, if it were not for the painful diligence of commentators, we
should hardly notice that line 45 is an absurd answer to Tityrus seeking
for his freedom.' In spite of such disconcerting perplexities, this poem
is one of the loveliest of the Eclogues.

MELIBOEUS. Tityrus, thou, reclined beneath the covert of a spreading beech,
Dost meditate a woodland melody on thy slender reed.
We, banished from the lands where we were born and our loved fields,
We from our homes are fleeing; thou, Tityrus, idling in the shade,
Art teaching these woods to resound 'beautiful Amaryllis!'
TITYRUS. O Meliboeus, a God is he who blessed us with this peace:
For as a God I'll always deem him; often from our folds
A tender lamb I'll choose to stain his altar with its blood.
Through his kind grace my herd may roam, as you behold, while I
May sit here with my rustic reed and pipe to my heart's content.　10
MELIBOEUS. I grudge you not, but marvel at your luck. Throughout the land
What hurry and tumult! Look how I myself, heart-sick, am driving
My goats along!—Here, Tityrus, is one I scarce can lead.

For there just now mid the dense hazels painfully she gave birth to twins,
The hope of the flock, ah! dropt and left upon the naked stone.
Often this misery was foretold me (I remember now)
By oaks struck with heaven's lightning—had not my wits been dull.
But come now, tell me, Tityrus, who is this God of yours?
TITYRUS. The town which men call Rome, Meliboeus, I, fool that I was,
Thought must be like this town of ours, whither we shepherd folk   20
Are often wont to drive the tender younglings of our flocks.
Just so I knew that puppies were like dogs, that new-born kids
Were like their dams; just so great things with small would I compare.
But this town has reared up her head among all other towns
As high as cypresses are wont among the bending osiers.
MELIBOEUS. And what cause could there be so great that you should
        visit Rome?
TITYRUS. My freedom, which, though late, yet looked with kind eyes on
        my sloth,
When already as I trimmed it my beard was falling whiter;
Yet kindly has it looked on me and come after long years,
Since Amaryllis has my heart and Galatea has left me.   30
For, now will I confess it, while Galatea ruled me,
No thought of savings could be mine, nor hope of liberty.
Though many was the victim that was led forth from my byres,
And many a rich cheese was pressed for the ungrateful town,
Yet never money-laden did I bring my wallet home.
MELIBOEUS. I used to wonder, Amaryllis, why you invoked the Gods
So sadly; for whom you left your apples hanging on their trees.
Tityrus was gone far from home. The very pine-trees, Tityrus,
Were calling for you, ay, the very brooks and copses yonder.
TITYRUS. What else was I to do? Where save at Rome might I escape   40
My slavery? Where else find Gods propitious to my prayer?
There it was, Meliboeus, I beheld that youth for whom
On twice six days of every year our festal altars smoke.
For there he was the first to give a response to my plea:
'Pasture your oxen as of old, my children; rear your bulls.'
MELIBOEUS. Happy old man! so still these lands shall be yours, and for you
Ample enough. Though everywhere crops up the naked stone,
And marshy pools with slime-born reeds encroach upon your pastures,

Yet shall no strange unwonted herb poison your pregnant ewes,
And no baneful contagion from a neighbouring flock shall harm them. 50
Happy old man! Here, wandering amid familiar streams
And beside sacred springs you shall delight in the cool shade.
Still as of old shall yonder hedge bordering your neighbour's land,
Whose willow-bloom Hyblaean bees are rifling, oft persuade you
With gently whispering leaves to welcome sleep; while there beneath
The steep rock shall the pruner fling his song on the breeze.
Still shall you listen to your darling pigeons' husky coo,
Nor shall the turtle cease his moaning from the lofty elm.
TITYRUS. Sooner, grown light as air, shall stags roam grazing in the sky,
And the seas leave their fishes stranded bare upon the shore, 60
Sooner, each o'er the other's frontier wandering, shall the German
Quench his thirst in the Tigris, or the Parthian in the Soane,
Than from my heart the vision of his countenance shall fade.
MELIBOEUS. But we far hence must travel, some to the parched Africans,
To Scythia some, or Crete where flows the swift stream of Oaxes,
Or to the Britons utterly sundered from all the world.
Ah, shall I ever, long years hence, gazing again upon my home,
My humble cottage with its turf-piled roof, look round me amazed
On what was once my kingdom—a few scanty ears of corn?
What! shall some godless soldier possess these well-tilled acres? 70
A barbarian these crops? To what a pass has civil strife
Brought our unhappy citizens! Have we for these men sown our fields?
Go now, Meliboeus, graft your pears, plant out your vines in rows!
Away, once happy flock! Let us be gone! Away my goats!
Never again shall I, outstretched within a fern-fringed cave,
Watch you where far away you are hanging on some bushy crag.
No more songs shall I sing; no more, my goats, with me to tend you
Shall you crop flowering cytisus and the willow's bitter shoots.
TITYRUS. Why could you not for this one night have rested here with me
On a green couch of leaves? For look, we have apples ripe for eating, 80
And mealy chestnuts, and no lack of cheeses newly pressed.
Already wreaths of smoke are rising over the farmhouse roofs,
And longer fall the shadows from the high mountain crests.

ECLOGUE II

ALEXIS

The Sicilian shepherd Corydon laments his hopeless passion for the
beautiful youth Alexis. Much of the poem is an imitation of the eleventh
Idyll of Theocritus, in which Polyphemus the Cyclops complains of the
indifference of Galatea to his love. This is generally thought to be the
earliest of the *Eclogues*.

Once Corydon the shepherd loved the beautiful Alexis,
The darling of his master; but in vain he hoped and wooed;
So naught else could he do but seek day by day the dense shade
Of the tall beeches. There alone uselessly would he fling
These uncouth monodies abroad to the senseless woods and hills.
　O cruel Alexis, for my songs do you not care at all?
Have you no pity then? At last to my death you will drive me.
Now even the beasts are searching for some coolness in the shade;
Now the green lizards even in the briars are lying hid;
And Thestylis for the reapers spent by the scorching heat　　　　10
Is pounding her strong-scented herbs of garlic and of thyme.
Yet with me, as I trace your footsteps, under the burning sun
The vineyards are re-echoing to the shrill grasshoppers.
Was it not easier to endure the fierce moods and the proud
Disdain of Amaryllis? Ay, and Menalcas too—
Brown though he was and dark of skin, while you are white and fair?
Ah, lovely boy, beware, nor trust too blindly in your bloom.
The white bindweed is left to fall; dark hyacinths are gathered.
　So you despise me, Alexis, and ask not what I am,
How rich in flocks, and what good plenty of snow-white milk is mine. 20
Over the hills of Sicily my lambs in hundreds roam;
In summer and in winter too never does fresh milk fail me.
Such songs I sing as Amphīon of Thebes was wont to sing
When he called home his cattle on Actaean Aracynthus.
　Nor am I so ill-favoured. On the shore, when the smooth sea
Lay wind-becalmed, of late I saw my face. Were you the judge,
Not Daphnis even would I fear, since the image never lies.

Oh would you but consent to dwell in comradeship with me
Amid these homely fields in lowly cots, and shoot the deer,
Or drive the kids together with a green switch of hibiscus,   30
With me here in the woods in piping you should rival Pan.
  Pan it was who first taught us how to join many reeds
With wax; Pan is the guardian of sheep and of their shepherds.
Nor would you think it time ill spent with a reed to chafe your lip.
To teach himself this art what pains did not Amyntas waste?
  A pipe is mine compacted of seven hemlock stalks,
Each of a different length, a gift which once Damoetas gave me,
And dying said, 'Henceforth its second master shall you be.'
So said Damoetas: envy filled the fool's heart of Amyntas.
  Moreover two young roebucks—dangerous was the valley   40
Wherein I captured them—their hides still sprinkled with white spots,
Drain a ewe's udders twice a day. These I am keeping for you.
Thestylis has been begging a long while to get them from me;
And she shall have them, since my gifts are worthless in your eyes.
  Ah, lovely boy, come hither: see, for you the nymphs are bringing
Lilies in full-heaped baskets; for you too the fair Naiad
Is gathering yellow wallflowers and flaunting poppy-heads,
And with them blends narcissus and sweet-scented fennel flowers.
Then, twining them with cassia and with other fragrant herbs,
She sets off the soft hyacinth with the golden marigold.   50
With my own hands I will pick apples from the quince tree, pale
With tender down, and chestnuts, which my Amaryllis loved.
Plums smooth as wax I'll add; this fruit shall have its honour too.
Then bays I'll pluck and myrtle to be neighbours in one nosegay,
For sweetly will they blend their odours when they are thus arrayed.
  Corydon! you are a clown. For gifts naught does Alexis care;
Nor, should you seek to rival him with gifts, would Iollas yield.
  Ah me, what have I done, poor wretch! Let loose among my flowers
In madness the south wind, and boars to befoul my pure springs!
  Whom do you flee? Ah fool! Even the Gods dwelt in the woods,   60
And Dardan Paris. In the cities she herself has built
Let Pallas dwell; to me beyond all else are the woods dear.
  The grim lioness hunts the wolf, the wolf himself the goat,
The wanton goat roams hunting for the flowering cytisus,

Corydon follows you, Alexis: each by his lust is led.
  See now the bullocks drag home by the yoke the hanging plough,
And the sun as it leaves the sky doubles the lengthening shadows;
Yet me love still is burning; for what limit can love know?
  Ah Corydon, Corydon, what is this strange madness that has seized you?
Upon the leafy elm trees your vines are but half-pruned.   70
Nay, why not rather set about plaiting with pliant reeds
And osier withes something at least that daily need requires?
Another Alexis will you find, if this one scorns your love.

ECLOGUE III

PALAEMON

A rustic singing-match between two shepherds. As in the fifth Idyll of
Theocritus, upon which this poem is modelled, the rivals spend some time
in lively banter of each other before beginning the contest. The eight lines
in which Virgil complements his patron Pollio and sneers at the contem-
porary poets, Bavius and Maevius, are an artistic blot upon this amusing
poem.

MENALCAS. Tell me, Damoetas, who is it owns this flock? Is it Meliboeus?
DAMOETAS. No; Aegon. Not long since Aegon entrusted it to me.
MENALCAS. Poor sheep, ever a luckless flock! So while your master's gone
Courting Neaera, still in dread lest she should love me best,
Twice every hour this shepherd, this hireling milks his ewes,
And the juice from the flock is stolen, from the lambs the milk.
DAMOETAS. You'd best be cautious how you fling such taunts at other men.
I know both who was with you, while the he-goats peered askance,
And in whose sanctuary you lay—but the easy Wood-nymphs laughed.
MENALCAS. That must no doubt have happened on the day when I was
        seen   10
With jealous knife hacking the elms and tender vines of Micon.
DAMOETAS. And it was here, beside the ancient beeches, that you broke
The bow and shafts of Daphnis; for you had been sore grieved,

Wicked Menalcas, when you saw them given to the boy;
And could you not have somehow harmed him, you'ld have died for spite.
MENALCAS. When thieves become so daring, what can poor masters do?
Did I not see you, ah you rascal! lying in wait to steal
That goat of Damon's, while his dog Lycisca barked like mad?
And when I shouted, 'Where's the fellow running? Tityrus,
Beware! Muster your flock', you stole from sight among the sedge. 20
DAMOETAS. What! When I had conquered him in song, was he not bound
To yield the he-goat which the music of my pipes had won?
Since you don't seem to know it, that goat was mine, as Damon
Himself confessed to me, but said he could not give it up.
MENALCAS. *You* conquer *him* in singing! Why, did you ever own
A wax-joined pipe? Were you not wont, you bungler, at the cross-roads
To murder a miserable tune upon a scrannel reed?
DAMOETAS. Well, will you put it to the proof what each of us can do
Singing in turn? I stake this heifer. Lest you refuse, I tell you
She comes twice to the milking-pail, and gives suck to two calves.   30
Now say, what will you wager, if you'll contend with me?
MENALCAS. I would not dare stake anything against you from the flock.
At home I have a father, and a harsh step-mother too;
And twice a day both count the flock, and one of them the kids.
But—and yourself you'll own it to be far the greater stake—
Since you're resolved upon this folly, then two beechen cups
I'll wager, the carved handiwork of divine Alcimedon;
Whereon a pliant vine, embossed by the skilled graver's tool,
Is entwined with the spreading clusters of the pallid ivy.
In the centre are two figures, Conon [1] and—who was the other?—   40
He who once mapped out for mankind the whole globe of the heavens,
What seasons should the husbandman observe, what the bent ploughman.
Never yet have I touched them with my lips, but keep them stored.
DAMOETAS. Why for me also has that same Alcimedon made two cups,
And has enwreathed their handles with soft acanthus leaves.
In the centre he set Orpheus, and the woods following him.
Never yet have I touched them with my lips, but keep them stored.
When once you've seen the heifer, you'll have no praise for the cups.

---

[1] A Greek astronomer. The other was probably Eudoxus of Cnidus.

MENALCAS. You shan't escape me. On any ground you choose, there will
    I meet you.
Let but our umpire be—ah, yonder look, Palaemon comes. 50
I'll see to it you in future challenge nobody to sing.
DAMOETAS. Nay, sing, if you have aught. With me there shall be no delay.
I will refuse no umpire. But hark you, friend Palaemon,
This is no trifling matter; give it your closest heed.
PALAEMON. Sing then, since we are seated on this soft grassy turf.
Green now grows every cornfield, now burgeons every tree,
Leafy now are the woods, now is the loveliest of the year.
Begin Damoetas; then must you, Menalcas, follow him.
Turn by turn shall you sing: alternate songs the Muses love.
DAMOETAS. Muses, from Jove do I begin: of Jove are all things full. 60
He cherishes the fruitful earth; he pays heed to my songs.
MENALCAS. And me Apollo loves; ever with me Apollo finds
Those gifts so dear to him, laurels and sweet-blushing hyacinths.
DAMOETAS. Galatea hits me with an apple—ah the wanton girl!—
And flees into the willows, but hopes to be seen first.
MENALCAS. But my Amyntas, my beloved, unbidden comes to me,
So that by now no better known is Delia to my dogs.
DAMOETAS. Gifts for my goddess have I found; for I myself have marked
Where stock-doves have been building, high up in the tall trees.
MENALCAS. What I could, I have sent the boy, ten golden apples plucked 70
From a wilding tree: tomorrow I will send as many more.
DAMOETAS. How many and what tender vows has Galatea made me!
To the ears of the Gods, ye winds, carry some part of them.
MENALCAS. What avails it, Amyntas, that in heart you scorn me not,
If you are hunting the wild boars, while I must watch the nets?
DAMOETAS. Send Phyllis to me, for today's my birthday feast, Iollas.
When I shall slay a heifer for the crops, then come yourself.
MENALCAS. Phyllis beyond all girls I love, for she wept when I left her,
And cried a lingering 'Farewell, farewell, my lovely Iollas'.
DAMOETAS. The wolf is baneful to the folds, rain-storms to the ripe crops, 80
To the trees the wild winds, to me the wrath of Amaryllis.
MENALCAS. A delight is moisture to the corn, to weaning kids the arbute,
The pliant willow to breeding ewes, to me Amyntas only.
DAMOETAS. To Pollio my Muse is dear, rustic though she be.

Pierian sisters, fatten for your votary a heifer.
MENALCAS. Pollio makes new songs himself. Fatten for him a bull
With a butting horn already and with hoofs that spurn the soil.
DAMOETAS. May he who loves you, Pollio, share the joys that are your lot:
For him let honey flow and the rough bramble bear him spice.
MENALCAS. May he who hates not Bavius, love your songs, Maevius, too, 90
Plough with a team of foxes and strive to milk he-goats.
DAMOETAS. You who are gathering flowers and low-growing strawberries,
Run, run, lads: a cold serpent is lurking in the grass.
MENALCAS. Beware, my sheep; go not too far: it is not safe to trust
The stream's bank. Look, the ram himself is drying his wet fleece.
DAMOETAS. Tityrus, from the river drive away the grazing goats.
When it's time, in the fountain I will wash them all myself.
MENALCAS. Lads, drive the sheep into the shade. Should the heat touch
      the milk,
As it did t'other day, in vain shall our palms press the teats.
DAMOETAS. Alas my bull, how lean he is among the juicy vetch! 100
The same love is the bane both of the herd and the herd's master.
MENALCAS. These sheep at least—nor is love the cause—can scarce cleave
      to their bones.
Some evil eye, it must be, has bewitched my tender lambs.
DAMOETAS. Tell me, in what land (and you shall be my great Apollo)
Not wider than three ells does the space of heaven extend?[1]
MENALCAS. Tell me, in what land grow flowers with the names of kings
Inscribed, and you shall have our Phyllis for your very own.
PALAEMON. It's not for me to settle so great a strife between you.
Both you and he are worthy of the heifer, and all those
Who either fear the sweets of love or feel its bitterness. 110
Close now the rills, my lads; enough the meadow-lands have drunk.

[1] No convincing answer to this riddle has been proposed. The second riddle refers
to the hyacinth, supposed to be marked with AI for Aias, or with Y for Hyacinthus.

ECLOGUE IV

POLLIO

This famous poem was fantastically believed by the early Christians, and throughout the Middle Ages, to be a Messianic prophecy of Christ. It certainly foretells a new Golden Age in the immediate future, and associates the development of this era with the birth and growth of a child. This child was probably Pollio's, who was then Consul. The boy was to rule the world (not presumably as Emperor, but as Consul) with the virtues inherited from his father.

Sicilian muses, sing we now a somewhat loftier strain.
Not all delight in orchards, nor in lowly tamarisks.
Of woods be our song; but let the woods be worthy of a consul.
   Now come is the last age foretold by the Cumaean Sibyl:
Born is the mighty cycle of the centuries once more.
Now returns the just Virgin,[1] the Saturnian reign returns:
Now a new race of mortals to earth from heaven descends.
But do thou, chaste Lucina, speed the birth of that child
Under whom first shall the iron brood cease, and a golden race
Spring up throughout the world. Thine own Apollo now is king.   10
While thou art consul, Pollio, shall this glory of the time
Enter upon his course, and the great months commence their march.
The lingering traces of our guilt under thine auspices
Shall vanish, and release the Earth from never-ceasing dread.
The life of Gods the boy shall share; heroes shall he behold
Mingling with Gods, and he himself by them shall be beheld,
And rule a world to which his father's virtues have brought peace.
   But for thee, child, the Earth untilled, as her first pretty gifts,
Shall put forth straying ivy and foxglove everywhere,
And arum lilies mingled with smiling acanthus flowers.   20
Unherded shall the goats bring home their udders swollen with milk,
Nor shall the cattle fear the mighty lion. Of themselves
From the ground whereon thou liest shall spring flowers for thy delight.
The serpent too shall perish, and the treacherous poison plant
No more be seen; on every soil Assyrian spice shall grow.
   But soon as thou canst read the glorious tales of ancient heroes,

[1] Justice, who left the earth during the iron age.

And the deeds of thy father, and so learn what virtue is,
Slowly shall the fields grow yellow with the waving corn,
And on the uncultured bramble shall hang the purple grape,
And honey-dew shall be distilled from the leaves of sturdy oaks.   30
Yet some few traces shall survive of our old sinfulness,
Which will tempt men to venture on the sea in ships, to gird
Cities with walls, and with the furrowing plough to cleave the earth.
Then shall be seen a second Tiphys,[1] and a second Argo
Shall carry chosen heroes; other wars too there will be,
And again great Achilles against Troy shall be sent.
Thereafter, when the ripening years have made of thee a man,
The trader even shall quit the sea; the ship of pine no more
Shall exchange merchandise: all things alike will all lands bear.
No more shall the earth endure the hoe, nor vines the pruning hook,   40
The sturdy ploughman now shall loose his oxen from the yoke.
Wool shall no more be taught to mock varied hues; but the ram
Of himself in the meadow, now to sweetly blushing purple
Shall change the colour of his fleece, and now to saffron yellow;
While scarlet, aided by no art, shall clothe the grazing lambs.
   'Run on through such great ages', to their spindles the Fates sang,
Chanting in concord with the fixed decree of Destiny.
      Enter on thy great honours—soon will the time be come—
Dear offspring of the Gods, thou mighty scion of Jupiter.
See how the universe is shaking with its vaulted mass,   50
The earth and the expanses of the sea and heights of heaven!
See how all things that are rejoice in this age that is dawning!
Oh then for me may the last years of a long life still linger,
And inspiration such as shall suffice to tell thy deeds.
Not Thracian Orpheus, not Linus should vanquish me in song,
Though a mother to the one gave help, a father to the other,
To Orpheus Calliopēa, to Linus comely Apollo.
Even Pan, should he contend with me, and Arcady be judge,
Even Pan, with Arcady for judge, would own that he was vanquished.
Begin, little boy, to recognise thy mother with a smile.   60
To thy mother ten months have brought long pains and weariness.
Begin, little boy. That child on whom his parents have not smiled,
No God deems worthy of his board, no Goddess of her bed.

[1] The helmsman of the Argo.

ECLOGUE V

DAPHNIS

The shepherds Menalcas and Mopsus engage in a friendly contest of song.
Mopsus laments the death of Daphnis, Menalcas sings of his deification.
In 42 B.C. the birthday of the deified Julius Caesar was celebrated; and
critics have found an allegorical reference to this in the death and apotheosis
of Daphnis. Though this may be true, it can have been of little importance
to Virgil, and must be of still less to us. The first nine lines of Menalcas's
song are in Virgil's greatest style; and the compliments paid to each other
by the shepherd poets are exquisitely beautiful. The scenery of the poem
is Theocritean.

MENALCAS. Mopsus, since we have chanced to meet, skilled masters both
 of us,
You at breathing into slender reeds, and I at singing verses,
Here mid these elms and hazels why should we not sit down?
MOPSUS. You are the elder: you must say what's best to do, Menalcas;
Whether we seek the shade that trembles at the Zephyr's breath,
Or choose the shelter of this cavern. See how the wild vine
With clusters straying here and there has overrun the cave.
MENALCAS. Among our hills Amyntas is your only rival now.
MOPSUS. Soon shall we see him challenge Phoebus for the prize of song.
MENALCAS. Begin first, Mopsus, if you have any love-songs for your
 Phyllis,   10
Or praises of our Alcon, or railleries against Codrus.
Begin. Tityrus will keep watch over the grazing kids.
MOPSUS. Well then this song, which t'other day upon the green beech-bark
I carved and set to music, marking words and tune in turn—
This I will try. Then do you bid Amyntas strive with me.
MENALCAS. As far as the lithe willow tree must yield to the pale olive,
Or as to crimson rose-bushes the lowly Celtic nard,
So far must Amyntas in my judgement yield to you.
But now, lad, let's have done with talk. Here we are in the cave.
MOPSUS *sings*. For Daphnis by a cruel death destroyed the Nymphs
 lamented.   20

Of their tears you were witnesses, ye hazels and ye streams;
While in her arms clasping her son's piteous corpse, the mother
Cried out upon the cruelty of the Gods and of the stars.
No herdsman, Daphnis, in those days would drive his kine to pasture
Or to the cool streams lead them; nor would any beast of the field
Quench its thirst in the river, or crop one blade of grass.
Of thee, Daphnis, the forests and the savage mountains tell
How even the lions of Africa made moan over thy death.
Daphnis it was who first taught men to yoke beneath the car
Armenian tigers, who ordained the thiasus of Bacchus, 30
And bade them twine soft leafage around their supple spears.
As to its elm the vine lends glory, to the vines their grapes,
As to the herds the bulls, as corn to rich tilth, so art thou
Thy people's only glory. Since the Fates took thee from us,
Even Pales, even Apollo have left desolate our fields.
Oft in the furrows, wherein we have sown big grains of barley,
Unfruitful darnel there springs up and sterile stalks of oat.
Where once soft violets nestled, or bright narcissus glowed,
The thistle rises and the thorn bristling with prickly spikes.
With leaves, ye shepherds, strew the ground, with shade o'ercanopy 40
The fountain; such the honours Daphnis wills that you should pay him.
Then build a tomb; and on the tomb let these lines be inscribed:
'I am Daphnis. From these woods my fame spread to the very stars.
Fair was the flock I shepherded, myself more fair than they.'
MENALCAS. Such a delight, thou godlike poet, is thy song to me
As, to the weary, slumber on the grass, as in noon's heat
With sweet water to quench one's thirst out of a gushing rill.
Not on the pipes alone you match your master, but in song.
Fortunate youth, now second to him only shall you be.
However to repay you I will sing as best I may 50
This song of mine, and will exalt your Daphnis to the stars.
To the stars will I lift him. Me too did Daphnis love.
MOPSUS. Could aught be more delectable than such a boon to me?
The youth himself was worthy to be honoured in your song;
And by Stimichon already we have heard your verses praised.
MENALCAS. Daphnis, transfigured, marvels at the unfamiliar threshold
Of Olympus, and beneath his feet beholds the clouds and stars.

Therefore throughout the woods and fields a frolic rapture reigns
Among Pan and the shepherds, and among the Dryad nymphs.
The wolf now plots no ambush for the flocks, and hunting-nets   60
No snare against the stag; for peace is dear to kindly Daphnis.
Even the unshorn mountains are flinging joyously
Their voices to the stars; the very rocks, the very trees
Break into singing: 'A God now, a God is he, Menalcas.'
Oh be thou kind and gracious to thine own. Behold four altars!
Two for thee, Daphnis; and these two for sacrifice to Phoebus.
Once every year two cups with fresh milk foaming, and two bowls
Filled with rich olive oil upon your altars will I set.
Above all, gladdening bounteously the feast with wine (in winter
Before the hearth, beneath the shade if it be harvest-time),   70
That new nectar from Chios out of flagons will I pour.
Their songs shall Lyctian Aegon and Damoetas sing to me,
While Alphesiboeus mimics the leaping Satyrs' gambols.
Evermore shall these rites be thine, both when to the Nymphs we pay
Our solemn annual vows, and when we purify our fields.
While the boar loves the mountain ridge, while the fish loves the stream,
While bees shall feed on thyme, and the cicadas drink the dew,
For so long shall thine honour, thy name and praise endure.
As to Bacchus and to Ceres, so to thee year by year
The husbandmen shall make their vows, and thou wilt grant their
          prayers.   80
MOPSUS. How, with what gifts can I repay you for so sweet a song?
For not the south wind's whisper as it rises, nor the waves
Breaking upon the shore can so delight me, nor the sound
Of rivers that run murmuring down from rocky glen to glen.
MENALCAS. Take first from me these fragile pan-pipes. It was they that
          taught me
'Once Corydon the shepherd loved the beautiful Alexis';
Taught me too 'Who's the owner of this flock? Is it Meliboeus?'
MOPSUS. But do you take this crook, my friend, which, oft as he begged
          it of me,
Antigenes could not win (he was worth loving in those days),
A lovely crook with even knots and ringed with brass, Menalcas.   90

ECLOGUE VI

VARUS

The sixth Eclogue begins with an address to Virgil's patron Varus, and then gives a charming description of the capture by two young shepherds (or, as some think, by two Satyrs) of the sleeping Silenus, whom they then persuade to sing to them a song about the creation of the world, followed by various mythological stories. The brief Lucretian cosmogony is superb poetry, and there are some lovely lines in the mythological tales; but there is no narrative interest, and the general effect is somewhat scrappy. The interview of the poet-soldier Gallus with Linus and the Muses seems out of harmony with the rest of the poem.

When she was young my rustic Muse disdained not to disport
In Syracusan verse, nor blushed in the greenwood to dwell;
But when of kings and battles I would sing, Apollo plucked
My ear and monished me: 'A shepherd, Tityrus, should feed
Sheep that are fat; but finely spun should be the song he sings.'
So now, Varus (since you will find poets enough, and more,
Eager to tell your praises and to chronicle sad wars),
Upon my slender pipe I'll brood over a sylvan theme.
I sing not without warrant: yet if some there be to read
And find charm in these poems, 'tis of thee my tamarisks   10
And all my woods shall sing. No page to Phoebus is more dear
Than that upon whose front the name of Varus is inscribed.
    Proceed, Pierian Muses. Young Chromis and Mnasyllos
Peering within a cavern found Silenus slumbering,
His veins swollen as ever with the wine of yesterday.
Not far from him lay garlands that had fallen from his head,
And grasped by its well-worn handle hung down his heavy jar.
They seize the old man and bind him (for with promise of a song
Oft had he cheated them) with chains from his own garlands made.
Aegle joins their company and cheers their fainting courage,   20
Aegle the loveliest of the Naiads. Wide-eyed now he stares,
While she with crimson mulberry juice is staining his brows and temples.

He smiling at their trickery cries, 'To what end tie these bonds?
Release me, boys. Enough that you have shown that you could bind me.
The songs you longed for you shall hear: songs shall be your reward;
For her payment in other kind'; and straightway he begins.
Then to the measure might you see Fauns dance and savage beasts
Gambol; then stubborn oak trees sway their tops to and fro.
No greater joy in Phoebus hath the Parnassian rock,
Nor to Ismarus and Rhodope is Orpheus such a marvel.   30
    For he sang how the seeds of earth and of air and of sea
And of the liquid fire of heaven, throughout the boundless void
Together congregated; how from these first elements
Came all beginnings, and the world's young orb grew to one mass;
Then how the land hardened its soil, and shut Nereus apart
Within the sea, and gradually assumed the forms of things.
And now Earth looks with wonder at the new Sun as he mounts
In splendour, and the rain-showers fall from the uplifted clouds;
When first began the forests to arise, and living things
Went wandering here and there over the hills that knew them not.   40
    Next of the stones that Pyrrha flung he tells; of Saturn's reign;
Of the vultures of Caucasus, and of Prometheus' theft.
Then he tells how on Hylas, lost within the fountain's depth,
The sailors called, till 'Hylas! Hylas!' all the shores resounded.
Then of Pasiphaë,[1] fortunate if no herds had ever been,
He sings how she found solace in her love for a snow-white bull.
Ah miserable maiden, what frenzy has seized on thee!
Proetus' daughters[2] filled the fields with counterfeited lowing;
Yet for a union so foul and monstrous, with a beast,
None of them longed; though for her neck each one had feared the yoke,   50
And many a time on her smooth brows had felt for budding horns.
Ah miserable maiden, now thou art roaming o'er the hills,
While he, couching his snowy flank upon soft hyacinths
Under a dark green ilex tree is chewing the pale grass,
Or following some heifer in the great herd. 'O ye Nymphs,[3]

---

[1] Wife of Minos king of Crete, lover of Poseidon's sacred bull, and mother of the Minotaur.
[2] The daughters of Proetus king of Argos were punished by Juno for their pride with madness, and imagined themselves to be cows.
[3] From here to line 60 Pasiphaë herself speaks.

Close, ye Nymphs of Dicte, close now the forest glades.
Might I not hope then that the footprints of my wandering steer
Would somewhere chance to meet my eyes? Or else may it not be
That by green herbage tempted, or following the herd,
Some heifers will escort him home to the Gortynian[1] stalls?'   60
    Then sings he of the maiden[2] whom those Hesperid apples charmed;
Then the sisters of Phaëthon with moss on a bitter bark
He enrings, and as tall alder trees raises them from the ground.
Then sings he of Gallus, as he roamed beside Permessus' stream;[3]
How one of the nine sisters led him to the Aonian hills,
And how to do him honour all the choir of Phoebus rose;
And how Linus the shepherd, master of godlike song,
His locks with flowers and bitter parsley garlanded, spoke thus:
'These pipes the Muses give thee—nay, take them—it was these
To the ancient bard of Ascra[4] once they gave; wherewith he charmed   70
Firm-rooted ash trees and would draw them down the mountain-sides.
With these the birth of the Grynēan forest[5] do thou tell,
That there may be no grove wherein Apollo glories more.'
    And then he sang of Scylla, of whom the tale is told
How with her white waist girdled with barking monsters foul,
She harried the Greek ships, and in the swirling waves, alas,
Her sea-dogs rent and swallowed the trembling mariners.
And last he told of Tereus[6] and his transfigured limbs,
Of that feast and that gift for him by Philomel prepared,
Of her swift flight to desert places, and (alas, poor wretch!)   80
How with the wings of a bird she flitted over her lost home.
    All these songs that in ancient days Apollo had rehearsed,
While happy Eurotas listened and taught them to his laurels,
Silenus sings; the echoing vales repeat them to the stars:
Till Vesper bade the shepherds drive the flocks into their folds
And tell their tales, as on he moved through an unwilling sky.

[1] Cretan.   [2] Atalanta.
[3] A Boeotian river near Mount Helicon.   [4] Hesiod.
[5] Grynium was an Aeolian town, sacred to Apollo.
[6] Tereus married Philomela, then pretended she was dead and married her sister
Procne. When she discovered the truth, Procne killed her sister's son Itys, and fled,
changed by the Gods to a swallow. Tereus was transformed into a hoopoe, Philo-
mela into a nightingale.

ECLOGUE VII

MELIBOEUS

This is a singing-match between Corydon the goatherd and the shepherd
Thyrsis, with Daphnis as umpire. Corydon wins; but it is not easy to
see why. 'Is it because Thyrsis is the more humorous and whimsical—
even perhaps, in his exaggerations, satirical?' (a marginal note in the
late Lascelles Abercrombie's Virgil). The poem, though full of remi-
niscences of Theocritus, is one of the most beautiful and perfect of the
Eclogues. The scenery is no-man's-land; Arcadian shepherds singing on
the banks of the Lombard Mincius, under the shade of Sicilian trees.

MELIBOEUS. Beneath a whispering ilex tree Daphnis had sat him down,
While Corydon and Thyrsis had driven their flocks together,
Thyrsis his sheep, and Corydon his goats with swollen udders,
Both in the flowering springtide of their youth, Arcadians both,
Ready as rivals in a match to sing and make reply.
Thither, while I was sheltering from the cold my tender myrtles,
Had strayed the he-goat of my flock—when whom should I catch sight of
But Daphnis?—who in turn caught sight of me; and 'Quick!' he cries,
'Come hither, Meliboeus; your goat and kids are safe;
And if you've time for idling, rest here beneath the shade.   10
Hither unherded will your steers come through the meads to drink;
Here Mincius flows, with slender rushes fringing his green banks,
And from the sacred oak tree comes the hum of swarming bees.'
What should I do? Neither a Phyllis had I, nor an Alcippe,
Whom I might trust to pen within their folds my new-weaned lambs.
And a great singing-match it was—Corydon against Thyrsis.
Yet a more urgent business than my work I deemed their play.
So in alternate verses did these two swains begin
Their contest: with alternate song the Muse inspired their minds.
These Corydon, those Thyrsis repeated each in turn.   20
CORYDON. Beloved Nymphs of Libethra, either grant me such a strain
As you gave to my Codrus; for *his* songs come most near
To Apollo's songs; or if such power be not for all of us,

Here on the sacred pine-tree my tuneful pipe shall hang.
THYRSIS. Ye shepherds of Arcadia, with wreaths of ivy crown
Your rising poet, that with envy Codrus's guts may burst.
Or, should he give me praise beyond my due, garland my brow
With foxglove, lest his evil tongue blast the outsetting bard.
CORYDON. This head of a bristling boar to thee, Diana, little Micon
Dedicates, and the branching antlers of a long-lived stag.   30
If such good fortune hold, why then at full length shalt thou stand
In smooth marble, thy ankles with purple buskins bound.
THYRSIS. A bowl of milk, Priapus, and these few cakes are all
That you can hope for yearly: poor is the garden you protect.
Now, for the time, of marble have we made you; but if soon
Prosperous births increase the flock, then shall you be of gold.
CORYDON. Galatea, child of Nereus, sweeter than Hybla's thyme,
More white and lustrous than a swan, lovelier than pale ivy,
Soon as the bulls are wandering home from pasture to their byres,
If still some love for him you feel, come to your Corydon.   40
THYRSIS. Nay, let me seem to you more bitter than Sardinian herbs,
More rough than butcher's broom, more vile than seaweed storm-upflung,
If this day seem not to me now longer than a whole year.
Go home, my well-fed steers; if you have any shame, go home!
CORYDON. Ye springs that gush through mosses, and you grass more soft
          than sleep,
And the green arbutus that shields you with its chequered shade,
Ward from my flock the noonday heat. Now come the parching days
Of summer; now the buds are swelling on the vine's glad shoots.
THYRSIS. Here is a hearth and resinous brands; here, a big fire that burns
All day and night, and doorposts black with never-failing soot.   50
Here we care less for the cold blasts of Boreas than the wolf
For a great throng of sheep, or rushing rivers for their banks.
CORYDON. Junipers here are standing, and prickly chestnuts too;
Everywhere strewn beneath each tree are lying their own fruits;
All things are smiling now: but if the beautiful Alexis
Came no more to these hills, you'd see the very streams run dry.
THYRSIS. Parched are the fields; the grass dies thirsting in the tainted air;
Liber has grudged to the bare hills the cool shade of his vines.
But if hither comes my Phyllis, all the trees will be green,

And the Sky-god in abundance shall descend in genial showers.   60
CORYDON. To Hercules the poplar is most dear, the vine to Bacchus,
Myrtles to lovely Venus, to Apollo his own laurel.
Phyllis loves hazels; and so long as Phyllis loves them, neither
By myrtle nor by laurel shall the hazels be outvied.
THYRSIS. In the woods comeliest is the ash, in the gardens the pine,
The poplar tree by rivers, on mountain heights the fir:
But if you, lovely Lycidas, would often visit me,
The ash should yield to you in the wood, in the gardens the pine.
MELIBOEUS. This I remember, and how Thyrsis, conquered, strove in
    vain.
From that day Corydon for us is Corydon indeed.   70

ECLOGUE VIII

PHARMACEUTRIA

This poem, which is one of the least successful of the *Eclogues*, begins
with a frigid little flattery of Pollio, after which the shepherds Damon and
Alphesiboeus each sing their songs, Damon personifying a rejected and
resentful wooer, and Alphesiboeus a woman forsaken by her lover, whom
she tries to recover by various enchantments, which in the end are
successful.

Damon's song consists largely of translations from Theocritus; but
there is one passage of which Macaulay writes: 'I think the finest lines
in the Latin language are those five which begin,

Saepibus in nostris parvam te roscida mala—

I cannot tell you how they struck me. I was amused to find that Voltaire
pronounces that passage to be the finest in Virgil.' Whatever we may
think of this somewhat impulsive judgement, it must, I think, be admitted
that Virgil has here far surpassed the lines of Theocritus which had in-
spired him (Theocritus, XI, 25–29).

All who have read the *Simaitha* of Theocritus, even in translation, will
agree that the song of Alphesiboeus is little more than a lifeless academic

imitation. Yet it has at least one passage of great and original beauty,
where the enchantress compares the longing of Daphnis to that of a lost
heifer, wearied with seeking her mate through the forest. The mention
of lynxes and of Mount Oeta shows that the scenery is not Italian.

The Muse of Alphesiboeus and of Damon, those two shepherds,
At whose melodious rivalry the heifer marvelling
Forgot to graze, and lynxes stood spell-bound at their song,
While rivers were enchanted and stayed their course—the Muse
Of Alphesiboeus and of Damon will I now rehearse.
   Whether, my friend, you are passing the rocks of great Timavus,
Or skirting the Illyrian coast—Ah will it ever come,
That day when freedom shall be mine to sing your noble deeds?
Will the day ever come when I may spread throughout the world
Your poems, alone worthy of the Sophoclean buskin?   10
With you I now begin, with you shall end. Accept these songs
At your bidding essayed, and suffer that about your brows
This creeping ivy be entwined mid your victorious laurels.
   Scarce had the cold shadow of night departed from the sky,
What time the dew on tender grass is sweetest to the flock,
When Damon leaning on a smooth olive-staff thus began.

DAMON

Rise, heralding the genial day, O Morning Star; while I,
Cheated in the love which Nysa my betrothed has spurned,
Make my complaint, and though their witness has availed me naught,
Yet, as I die, invoke the Gods in this my latest hour.   20
   Your melodies of Maenalus[1], my flute, begin with me.
Ever with rustling forests and with whispering pine trees clad
Is Maenalus; ever to the loves of shepherds doth he listen,
And to Pan who first bade the idle reeds be dumb no more.
   Your melodies of Maenalus, my flute, begin with me.
Nysa weds Mopsus. What strange loves may we not look for now?
Griffins shall mate with mares, and we shall live to see some day
The timorous deer flocking to drink together with fierce hounds.

[1] A mountain in Arcadia.

Your melodies of Maenalus, my flute, begin with me.
Mopsus, new torches you must cut: for you the bride they are bringing. 30
Scatter nuts,[1] bridegroom: for you Hesperus rises over Oeta.
    Your melodies of Maenalus, my flute, begin with me.
O wedded to a worthless lord! You who have scorned all men,
You that have ever hated my pan-pipes and my goats,
Hated these shaggy eyebrows and this unkempt beard of mine,
Who think there is no God that heeds the falsities of mortals!
    Your melodies of Maenalus, my flute, begin with me.
Within our orchard I first saw you plucking dewy apples,
A small girl with my mother: it was I was your guide.
My eleventh year was over; I was entering on the next: 40
Already from the ground the fragile branches I could touch.
Oh then I saw, and straight was lost, and fatal folly engulfed me.
    Your melodies of Maenalus, my flute, begin with me.
Now I know what Love is: upon their hard and flinty crags
Either Tmaros or Rhodope, or the farthest Garamantes
Gave birth to him, a boy not of our race nor of our blood.
    Your melodies of Maenalus, my flute, begin with me.
Merciless Love could teach a mother to pollute her hands
With her own children's blood. O mother, cruel wast thou too.
Was the mother more cruel, or more wicked was that boy?   50
Wicked was he; but cruel, O mother, wast thou too.
    Your melodies of Maenalus, my flute, begin with me.
Now let the wolf flee from the sheep; let rugged oaks bear fruit
Of golden apples; let the alder with narcissus bloom;
Let tamarisks distil rich drops of amber from their bark;
Let owls too vie with swans, and let Tityrus be an Orpheus,
An Orpheus in the woods, among the dolphins an Arion!
    Your melodies of Maenalus, my flute, begin with me.
Let the whole earth become mid sea! Farewell, ye woods, farewell!
From some aerial mountain-crag headlong will I plunge down   60
Into the waves: accept thou that as my last dying gift.
    Break off your songs of Maenalus, my flute, now break them off.

---

[1] He was to fling away nuts among his boy-companions, to show that his boyish
games were over.

Thus Damon. Now, what answering song Alphesiboeus sang
Tell, ye Pierian Muses. We cannot all do all things.

ALPHESIBOEUS

Go, bring me water; next enwreathe this altar with soft wool;
Then burn these juicy herbs and leaves, and this male frankincense;
That I may try by magic rites to turn my lover's mood
From sanity to frenzy. Naught is lacking here save charms.
   Draw him home from the town, my charms, draw Daphnis home to me.
The charm of song can even draw the moon down from the sky;   70
By Circe's charms the comrades of Ulysses were transformed.
Chanting will burst asunder the cold serpent in the meadows.
   Draw him home from the town, my charms, draw Daphnis home to me.
Around you first three threads, each of three different colours twined,
Thus do I tie, and thrice about this altar do I draw
Your image. In odd numbers doth the God take delight.
   Draw him home from the town, my charms, draw Daphnis home to me.
In three knots, Amaryllis, three colours must you twine.
Quick, Amaryllis, twine them and say, 'The bonds of Love I am twining.'
   Draw him home from the town, my charms, draw Daphnis home
     to me.   80
As this clay hardens and this wax melts in the selfsame fire,
Even so may Daphnis harden and melt for love of me.
Now sprinkle meal and kindle the crackling bays with pitch.
Me cruel Daphnis burns: I against Daphnis burn this laurel.
   Draw him home from the town, my charms, draw Daphnis home to me.
May such love possess Daphnis as when a heifer, wearied
With searching vainly for her mate through thickets and deep woods,
Upon the margin of a brook sinks down in the green sedge,
Forlorn, nor minds she night's late hour that warns her to depart—
May such love seize him, and to heal it naught at all may I care.   90
   Draw him home from the town, my charms, draw Daphnis home to me.
These relics that perfidious man left with me not long since,
Dear pledges of himself; which now, under my very threshold,
O Earth, to thee will I commit. These pledges owe me Daphnis.
   Draw him home from the town, my charms, draw Daphnis home to me.

These herbs, these poisons, that were culled in Pontus, it was Moeris
Himself who gave them me. Such herbs are common weeds in Pontus.
Oft by their sorcery have I seen Moeris turn wolf and hide
Within the woods, oft call forth spirits from their deep-dug graves,
And charm away to other fields whole harvests of sown corn.   100

    Draw him home from the town, my charms, draw Daphnis home to me.
Amaryllis, carry these ashes forth and into a running stream
Over your head fling them, and look not back. With these will I
Afflict Daphnis. Naught cares he for the Gods, naught for my charms.

    Draw him home from the town, my charms, draw Daphnis home to me.
Look, of itself the ash, while we delay to carry it hence,
Has kindled the altar with a flickering flame. Good be the omen!
Something it must be—and there is Hylax barking at the threshold.
Can I believe it? or do lovers cheat themselves with dreams?

    Break off! Daphnis from town is coming. Break off now, my
      charms!   110

ECLOGUE IX

MOERIS

The historical background of this poem is the same as that of the first
Eclogue. Menalcas is certainly meant to be Virgil, and Moeris seems to
be his farm-servant; but whether Menalcas has been expropriated from
his farm, or is still in possession of it, is by no means clear. Various
explanations have been proposed, but none are convincing. Two of the
passages quoted from the poetry of Menalcas are translated from Theo-
critus.

LYCIDAS. Whither are you off to, Moeris? To the town, as the path leads?
MOERIS. O Lycidas, we have lived to see the day when—such a thing
We never feared—when a stranger, lord of our little farm,
Can say, 'Mine is this homestead. You old tenants, begone.'
Now beaten and despairing (since chance rules all things here)
To him we are carrying these kids—and a foul curse go with them!
LYCIDAS. Yet surely I had heard that from the place where yonder hills

Begin to retire, descending hither in a gentle slope,
Down to the stream and those old beeches with their shattered tops,
By his songs your Menalcas had saved that whole domain. 10
MOERIS. So you had heard, and so said rumour. But among martial arms
These songs of ours, good Lycidas, are of no more avail
Than, as they say, Chaonian doves beneath the swooping eagle.
Had not a raven on my left from the hollow ilex tree
Forewarned me to cut short this new dispute as best I might,
Neither had I, your Moeris, been alive, nor yet Menalcas.
LYCIDAS. Alas, of such a crime who could be guilty? Alas, Menalcas,
So nearly did we lose you and the solace that you gave us!
Who would there be to sing the Nymphs? Who then would strew the
     ground
With flowers and herbage, or embower the springs with a green shade?[1] 20
Who'ld sing those songs which t'other day I slyly caught from you
When you were on your way to visit our darling Amaryllis?
'Till I return (the way is short), Tityrus, feed my goats,
And, when fed, drive them, Tityrus, to water; and as you drive them
Beware, get out of the he-goat's way; he'll butt you with his horn.'
MOERIS. Or these lines, yet unfinished, of the song he made for Varus:
'Varus, thy name—if only our dear Mantua be spared,
Mantua, alas, too near a neighbour to ill-starred Cremona—
Thy name her swans shall bear aloft to the stars in their song.'
LYCIDAS. As you would have your swarms of bees avoid the bitter yew, 30
And your kine swell their udders browsing on cytisus,
Begin, if you have aught to sing. Me too have the Muses made
A poet; I too have my songs: yes, even I am called
A singer by the shepherds, but I heed not what they say.
For surely naught have I yet sung worthy of Varius
Or of Cinna, a mere cackling goose among melodious swans.
MOERIS. That's what I'm trying, Lycidas, silently running through it—
If memory will but serve me. And no mean song it is.—
'Come hither, Galatea! In the waves what sport can be?
Here spring is glowing; here beside the rivers Earth pours forth 40
Her varied flowers; here the white silver poplar overhangs
The cavern, and the trailing vines weave bowers of cool shade.

[1] A reference to Eclogue v, 40.

Come hither! Let the raging waves dash themselves on the shore.'
LYCIDAS. What was it I heard you singing all alone on that clear night?
The melody I remember, could I but recall the words.
MOERIS. 'Daphnis, why art thou gazing at the ancient risings of the signs?
Look how the star of Caesar,[1] child of Venus, has advanced—
The star whose influence will make the fields rejoice with corn,
And on the sunny hills the colour deepen on the grape.
Graft thy pears, Daphnis; by thy children's children shall their fruit be
    plucked.'   50
Time takes from us all things, the mind even. How often, I remember,
In boyhood I would lay to rest the summer suns with song.
Forgotten now are all my many songs. Nay, his voice even
Is taking leave of Moeris. Wolves have seen Moeris first.[2]
Yet those songs will Menalcas sing you often as you will.
LYCIDAS. How long with your excuses will you baffle my desire?
But now the sea is silent. How smooth and still it lies!
Every breath, every murmur of the wind is fallen dead.
Just here is half our journey; for, see, Bianor's tomb
Is at last coming into view. There, where the husbandmen   60
Are stripping the dense foliage, there, Moeris, let us sing.
Put down the kids here: we shall still have time to reach the town.
Or if we fear lest night should first bring on a storm of rain,
We may go singing all the way; for so the road's less irksome.
Come, that we may go singing, I'll relieve you of your burden.
MOERIS. Say no more, lad; let us think only of the task before us.
Our songs we'll sing far better when he himself is come.

[1] The comet which appeared soon after Julius Caesar's death.
[2] It was believed that, if a wolf saw you before you saw him, you would be struck
dumb.

ECLOGUE X

GALLUS

This Eclogue, probably composed in 37 B.C., is the latest in date of the collection. Cornelius Gallus (an important soldier and politician, a distinguished elegiac poet, and the lover of a celebrated actress, the freed-woman Cytheris) is imagined to be lying under a rock in Arcadia, wasted away by his passion for Lycoris (the literary name of Cytheris), and comforted by the sympathy of shepherds and swineherds, and of various Gods, Apollo, Silvanus and Pan. Gallus replies to them in a pathetic, but somewhat incoherent speech of great poetic beauty, inviting his truant Lycoris to come and live a life of pastoral felicity with him in Arcadia. It does not seem that Gallus really intends to die for love, as did Daphnis in the first Idyll of Theocritus, upon which the whole scene is closely modelled. Though this is in some ways the most artificial of all the Eclogues, there is perhaps as much beautiful poetry in it as in any other.

This last task, Arethusa,[1] vouchsafe me: a brief song
Must I sing for my Gallus, yet such as his Lycoris
Herself may read. To Gallus who would refuse a song?
So never, when thou glidest neath the Sicilian waves,
May the sea intermingle its briny streams with thine—
Begin: of the unhappy love of Gallus let us sing,
While in the copse the blunt-nosed goats are browsing the tender leaves.
We sing not to the deaf; the woods re-echo every note.
    Where were you, in what forests and what glens, ye virgin Naiads,
When for an unrequited love Gallus lay perishing?   10
For neither on the highlands of Parnassus were you tarrying,
Nor upon Pindus, nor beside Aonian Aganippe.
For him even the laurels wept, even the tamarisks;
For him, as in the shadow of a lonely rock he lay,
Pine-shouldering Maenalus and the crags of cold Lycaeus wept.

[1] Invoked as the Sicilian Muse of pastoral poetry. For the myth of Arethusa and Alpheus, see Shelley's poem *Arethusa*.

The sheep too stand around (of us shepherds they think no shame;
Then do thou, divine poet, think no shame of thy flock:
Even beautiful Adonis pastured sheep beside the streams),
And with them came their shepherd; slowly came the swineherds;
And wet from gathering mast in wintry storms Menalcas came.   20
All of them asked, 'This love of thine, whence is it?' Came Apollo:
'Gallus, art thou not mad?' says he. 'Lycoris, thy sweet plague,
Is following some new lover through snows and through fierce camps.'
And next Silvanus came, his head with rustic honours decked,
Great lilies and tall fennel flowers that nodded as he went.
Pan came, the God of Arcady; with our own eyes we saw him,
Crimson with vermilion and with blood-red elderberries.
'Is there to be no end?' said he. 'Love recks not of such things.
Neither with tears may cruel Love be sated, nor the grass
With runnels, nor with cytisus the bees, nor goats with leaves.'   30
But sadly he answered, 'None the less, Arcadians, you will sing
My story to your mountains—you, Arcadians, alone skilled
In singing. Oh how sweetly would then my bones repose,
If one day to the music of your pipes you told my love.
Ah would I had been one of you, had either shepherded
One of your flocks, or been a dresser of your ripening vines!
Then, whether Phyllis or Amyntas, or whoever else
Might be my passion (what though brown be the beauty of Amyntas?
Dark of hue is the violet, and dark the hyacinth),
With me beneath a creeping vine they'ld lie among the willows: 40
Phyllis would cull me garlands, his songs would Amyntas sing.
Here are cool springs, Lycoris, here soft meadows, here are woods,
Here at thy side by time alone would life be worn away.
But now mad love for the stern God of battle keeps me in arms
Amid the threatening weapons of encircling foes; while thou
Far from thy homeland (would I might believe such tales untrue!)
On Alpine snows art gazing, and on the frost-bound Rhine,
Alone without me, O heartless one! Ah may those frosts not harm thee!
Ah may not the sharp ice ungently cut thy tender feet!
    But now those songs, that in Chalcidian[1] verses I composed,   50
I'll set them to the tunes of a Sicilian shepherd's pipe.

[1] Gallus had translated or imitated the poems of Euphorion of Chalcis.

I am resolved: within the woods and among wild beasts' dens
There do I choose to suffer. On the bark of tender trees
I'll carve my love. As the trees grow, with them shall grow my love.
Meanwhile companioned by the Nymphs I'll roam o'er Maenalus,
And to the death hunt savage boars. No frosts shall hinder me
From girdling with my hounds the glens of wild Parthenius.
What rapture to be speeding over rocks, through echoing woods!
To shoot Cydonian arrows from my Parthian bow, what joy
Were that!...Ah no, what folly! Vain are such cures to heal   60
My frenzy; as if that God could learn to pity human woes.
Now once again neither may woodland Nymphs, nor even songs
Delight me; even ye forests, once again fare you well.
By no hardships and miseries of ours may Love be changed,
Not though in winter's midst we drink of the icy stream of Hebrus,
Or battle with Sithonian snows and stormy sleet; not though,
When on the lofty elm the bark is parched to death, we drive
Flocks of Aethiopian sheep beneath the star of Cancer.
Since Love can vanquish all things, let us too yield to Love.'
    But now enough, Muses divine, your poet will have sung,   70
While he sits weaving baskets of slender hibiscus twigs.
These songs of mine see that you make of highest worth to Gallus,
Gallus, for whom my love is growing hour by hour more fast
Than shoots of the green alder in the early days of spring.
Rise now: for singers dangerous is the shade; most dangerous
The juniper: nay to the corn the evening shades are hurtful.
Go home, my well-fed goats—Hesperus rises—get you home.

PART II THE GEORGICS

INTRODUCTION

Until I had actually found myself translating the first lines of the *Georgics*, it had been my belief that of all poems they were the most impossible to translate. Indeed I am still far from sure that I was not right. For if there be such a thing as pure poetry, that is just what the *Georgics* so pre-eminently are; and the purer poetry is, the more untranslatable it is likely to be. It is true that almost every line of Virgil has a quite definite and ascertainable meaning, and is often a plain, even prosaic, statement of fact. But interesting as the meaning may be in itself, it contributes very little to the beauty of the poetry. Lucretius is a greater poet than the writer of the *Georgics*; but his work is less purely poetical, in the sense that it mattered very much indeed to him (and matters very much now to those who read him) what was the philosophical or ethical purport of every line he wrote. In this respect Lucretius was not unlike Wordsworth; while Virgil may perhaps be compared with such otherwise very different poets as Milton and Spenser, whose primary concern was with beauty of texture, felicity of phrasing, movement, imagery, and metrical subtlety; whereas Lucretius and Wordsworth, though at their happiest moments supreme masters of their art, were always consciously inspired by the moral and philosophical truth of what they were labouring to express.

I have myself translated Lucretius, and have found it possible to be almost as rigorously accurate in regular English blank verse as in prose; but I know well enough that the power and grandeur of his hexameters must have been sadly diminished in my translation. Much more must this be so in the case of such a purely poetical writer as Virgil, in whom the physical beauty and majestic sonority of the verse is everything, or nearly everything. In the more didactic and matter of fact parts of the poem, where the subject-matter still has a certain interest for us, some measure of success should be possible; but I doubt whether any English version, however skilful, could do more than imperfectly suggest the splendour of the exordium, with its long list of deities invoked, and its extravagant adulation of the divine Augustus; or the fantastic absurdities of the opening of the third book. Such themes have little more than a historical interest for us, if it were not for the magic of Virgil's poetry.

My chief reason for choosing ten-syllabled blank verse is that of all English metres it is the subtlest and most plastic, and so the least likely to impede and disturb the flow of Virgil's artfully inter-related sentences; for, as with all the greatest poets, mastery of movement comes first in importance. Unfortunately a line for line translation has seldom been possible,[1] as it would have been if I had used a fourteen-syllable line, or attempted some kind of English hexameter. But I have occasionally helped myself out of difficulties by venturing on a twelve-syllabled alexandrine, which, to my ear, has the same rhythmic character as a normal deca-syllabic line, if a strong medial caesura after the sixth syllable be avoided.

> And you, Liber
> And kindly Ceres, by whose bounty earth exchanged
> Chaonian acorns for the rich ear of corn,
> And blended with pure water of the stream
> The new-found grape; and you Fauns, present deities
> Of country folk. . . .

In these lines I do not feel the essential character and flow of the metre to be injured by the extrametrical 'exchanged', or by the last two syllables of 'deities'.

This quotation will also illustrate Virgil's inveterate love of far-fetched ornamental adjectives of place. Acorns are

---

[1] For this reason the numbering of the lines refers to the Latin lines, not to those of the translation.

'Chaonian', because the famous oak-groves of Dodona were in Chaonia. In the next line I have taken the liberty to substitute 'pure water from the stream' for 'Acheloea', an absurdly artificial synonym for water, derived from Acheloüs, the largest river in Greece. Virgil was indeed a consummate master of diction; but it was often what is now called 'poetic diction'. Thus a snake is usually 'black', that is 'deadly' (*ater*); the sea is 'immense'; the crops are 'glad' (*laetus*); and the epithet *magnus* is used almost as indiscriminately as was καλός by Theocritus. Yet Virgil's diction for the most part, though 'poetic', is by no means conventional, but chosen with exquisite judgement and felicity. Though perfection of movement may be the greatest quality of his poetry, the choice of appropriate diction is the most arduous problem in the task of a translator.

Virgil composed the four Books of the *Georgics* between 37 B.C. (the year when the *Eclogues* were published) and 30 B.C. They were dedicated to Maecenas, at whose request Virgil says that he undertook the task.

THE GEORGICS

BOOK ONE

What makes the cornfields glad, beneath what star,
Maecenas, it is well to turn the soil,
And wed the vine to the elm, how to tend oxen,
For nurturing flocks and herds what care is needful,
For keeping thrifty bees what knowledge, now
Shall I essay to sing. O ye most glorious
Lights of the universe, that lead along
Through heaven the gliding years; and you, Liber
And kindly Ceres, by whose bounty earth exchanged
Chaonian acorns for the rich ear of corn,
And blended with pure water from the stream
The new-found grape; and you Fauns, present deities   10
Of country folk (draw near together, Fauns
And Dryad maidens), it is your gifts to men
I sing. And thou, O Neptune, for whom earth,
Smitten by thy mighty trident, first sent forth
The neighing horse; and thou too, Genius of the groves,[1]
For whom three hundred snow-white steers roam grazing
Through Cea's fertile woodlands; and thou, Pan,
Guardian of flocks, leaving thy native forests
And the glades of Lycaeus, come, O Lord
Of Tegea, as thou lovest thine own Maenalus,[2]
Come hither of thy grace; Minerva too,
Inventress of the olive, and that youth[3]
Who showed to men the use of the bent plough;
And thou, Silvanus,[4] bearing in thy hand
A young uprooted cypress; and all you Gods   20

[1] Aristaeus, a bucolic demigod, whose story is told in the fourth Georgic.
[2] Lycaeus and Maenalus are mountains in Arcadia.
[3] Triptolemus.   [4] The Latin forest-god.

And Goddesses, who lovingly protect our fields,
Foster the unsown saplings, or send down
From heaven plenteous rain-showers on our crops;
And above all thou, Caesar,[1] of whom we know not
What company of the Gods shall some day claim thee;
Whether it be thy pleasure to frequent
Our cities and keep watch over our lands;
That so the mighty globe may welcome thee
As giver of increase, ruler of the seasons,
And with thy mother's myrtle wreathe thy brows;
Whether thou come as God of the vast sea,
And only to thy deity mariners pray,
While farthest Thule owns thee for her lord,   30
And Tethys[2] with the dower of all her waves
Buys thee to wed her daughter; or wouldst thou rather
Shine forth amid the lagging monthly Signs
A new star, where between Erigone[3]
And the pursuing Claws a space is opening—
The fiery Scorpion, see, draws in his arms
Leaving thee more than a just share of heaven—
Whatever thou wilt be (for Tartarus hopes not
For thee as king; may no such dread desire
Of sovereignty allure thee; albeit Greece
Is charmed by the Elysian fields, and Proserpine,
Reclaimed, cares not to follow her mother home);
Grant me an easy course; to my bold venture   40
Nod thy assent, and pitying with me
The rustics ignorant of the way, begin
Thy task, and learn even now to accept our prayers.

In early Spring, when the ice and snow are melting
On the white mountains, and the softening clod
Crumbles beneath the zephyr, then already
Let my bull groan dragging the deep-driven plough,
And the share glisten, scoured bright by the furrow.
That land alone answers the frugal farmer's prayer,

[1] Caesar Augustus.   [2] The wife of Oceanus.
[3] Erigone, or the Virgin, and the Scorpion are Signs of the Zodiac.

Which twice has felt the sun and twice the frost.
From it will boundless harvests fill the barns.
Yet ere with iron we cleave an unknown plain,   50
Let it be first our care to learn the wind
And the sky's changeful mood; the wonted tillage
And nature of the soil; what each field bears
Or will not bear: in this place corn, in that
More bountifully the grape will grow; elsewhere
Young trees shoot up and green grass spreads unbidden.
See you not how from Tmolus[1] fragrant saffron
Is sent to us, from India ivory,
Frankincense from the soft Sabaean Arabs;
But iron comes to us from the naked Chalybes,
From Pontus fetid beaver's oil, swift mares
From Epirus, winners of the Olympian palm?
These laws and these eternal covenants   60
Did Nature impose on certain lands, when first
Deucalion into the empty world flung stones,
Whence men were born, a stone-hard race. Come therefore,
Where the earth's loam is rich, let your strong oxen
Upturn it straightway in the year's first months,
And there let the clods lie for dusty summer
To bake them with the ripe heat of her suns.
But should the land be unfruitful, it will suffice,
Not long before the rising of Arcturus,
To lift it lightly with a shallow furrow,
That in your fertile acres weeds choke not
Your thriving crops; or, where the land is poor,
The scant moisture leave not your thin soil barren.   70
    But in alternate years you will allow
Your reaped fields to lie fallow, and the soil
To be left idle and strengthen with repose;
Or under another star sow yellow spelt
In fields whence you have carted many a load
Of beans rejoicing in their rattling pods,

[1] A mountain in Lydia.

Or a crop of slender vetch, or brittle haulm
And rustling undergrowth of bitter lupine.
But a crop of flax parches the ground; oats too
Parch it, and poppies steeped in Lethaean slumber.
Yet even these, planted alternately,
Need but light labour; only be not ashamed
To feed the dry soil with rich dung, and scatter   80
Grimy ashes over your exhausted fields.
Thus too with change of culture the land rests,
Nor meanwhile is the earth unploughed and thankless.
Often is it useful to fire barren fields,
And burn up the light stubble in crackling flames;
Whether it be that so the soil derives
Mysterious strength and fertile nutriment;
Or else that all its vices are by the fire
Baked out, and useless moisture sweated from it;
Or that the heat opens fresh paths and hidden pores
By which the sap may reach the tender blades;   90
Or rather that it hardens the loose soil
And narrows its wide cracks, lest searching rain-showers
And the fierce tyranny of the scorching sun
Or the north wind's piercing cold should sear and wither it.
　　Much in truth does he benefit the land
Who with the hoe breaks up the sluggish clods,
And harrows them with wattles (approvingly
Will golden Ceres watch him from high Olympus);
He too who turns his plough and again crosswise
Breaks through the ridges which he raised when first
He clove the soil. Thus evermore he disciplines
The ground, and gives his orders to the fields.
　　For rainless winters should a farmer pray,   100
And for moist summers. Winter dust makes glad
The corn, and glad the soil. Under no tillage
Does Mysia so vaunt herself, nor ever
At her own crops does Gargarus so marvel.[1]

[1] As after a wet summer and dry winter.

What praise is not his due who flings the seed,
Then grappling in close combat with the soil
Lays low the hillocks of unfertile sand;
Next from the stream brings water to his crops,
Guiding the rills; and when the scorched land swelters,
And the green blades are perishing, lo, from the brow
Of the hillside it traverses, he charms
A runnel forth, which as it gurgles down
Rouses mid the smooth pebbles a hoarse murmur,
And cools the parched fields with its gushing flow?   110
And what of him who, lest the stalk should droop
Beneath heavy ears, while yet the blade is tender,
Grazes down his luxuriant crop, so soon
As it grows even with the furrow's height?
Or of him who draws off the gathered moisture
Of marshy ground by drains of thirsty sand,
Then chiefly when in months of changeful weather
Some brimming river overflows and coats
Everything far and wide with mud, that so
With tepid moisture ditch and hollow steam?

  Nor yet, though men and oxen with long toil
Labouring the earth, have learnt these lessons well,
Does the nefarious goose commit no mischief,
Or the Strymonian cranes, or bitter-fibred   120
Succory; nor harmless is the shade of trees.
It was the Father himself willed that the path
Of husbandry should not be smooth: and he
First taught the art and skill to work the fields,
Sharpening men's wits by cares; nor would he suffer
His realm to drowse in heavy sluggishness.
Before Jove's reign no farmers tamed the land:
Nor was it lawful even to mark out
Or to divide the plain with boundary stones.
Men gathered for the common store; and Earth
Created all things of her own accord
More liberally when no one begged for gifts.
Jove it was who with deadly poison armed

Fell snakes, bade wolves to plunder, seas to swell,   130
Who from the leaves shook down the honey-dew,
Hid fire from men's eyes, and stopped the flow
Of wine that ran in rivers everywhere;
So that experience might by taking thought
Little by little hammer out divers arts,
Might seek the corn-blade in the furrowed earth,
And from the flint's womb strike the hidden fire.
Then first did rivers feel the hollowed alder;
Then did the sailor number and name the stars,
The Pleiades, the Hyades, and Arctos,
Bright daughter of Lycaon;[1] then they learnt
How to snare beasts in toils, and cheat with bird-lime,
And how to encircle the great glades with hounds: 140
And now one from the bank of a broad river
Flings out his net, seeking the depths, another
Drags along through the sea his dripping seine.
Then came the strength of iron, and the shrill saw-blade
(For the earliest men would split the fissile timber
With wedges); then came other various arts.
Mastery in all things stubborn labour gave them,
And the urgency of want when life was hard.
  Ceres it was who first taught men to turn
The earth with iron, when in the sacred wood
Acorns and arbutes failed them, and Dodona
Refused them food. Upon the corn too next   150
Fell trouble, when foul blight devoured the stalks,
And o'er the fields bristled the lazy thistle;
The crops perish, a prickly growth springs up,
Caltrops and burs, and mid the shining corn
Pestilent darnel and barren oats hold sway.
Therefore unless your hoe continually
Assaults the weeds, and your voice scares the birds,
Or if you prune not with your knife the leaves
Whose shade darkens your land, and in your prayers

---

[1] Callisto, beloved by Jupiter, and therefore turned into a bear by Juno.

Invoke not rain, alas, in vain will you envy
Your neighbour's big crop, and to solace hunger
Will go to shake down acorns from the oak-wood.
   Now must I name the hardy peasant's weapons,   160
Without which neither could the crops be sown
Nor raised: the share first and the heavy beam
Of the bent plough, and the Eleusinian Mother's[1]
Slow-rolling waggons, spiked sledges and drags
For threshing grain, and hoes of cruel weight;
Moreover the cheap wicker ware of Celeus,
Hurdles of arbute and the mystic fan
Of Iacchus. All these you must heedfully
Provide and long beforehand store them up,
If you would share the divine country's glory
In worthy measure. First in the woods an elm,
Bent by main force and trained to form the stock
Receives at length the shape of the curved plough.   170
Into the root of this a pole is fitted
Eight feet in length, two mould-boards and a share-beam
With double ridge. Also a light linden
Should have been felled for the yoke, and a tall beech
For a handle that can govern from the rear
The whole plough; and this timber should be hung
Above the hearth for the smoke to season it.
   Many are the precepts of our ancestors
I can repeat, unless you be reluctant
To lend attention to such trivial cares.
First of all must the threshing-floor be levelled
With a huge roller, kneaded with the hand,
And so made solid with tenacious clay,
Lest weeds spring up, or lest conquered by heat   180
It gape in cracks; for then plagues of all kinds
Will mock your toil. Often beneath the ground
The tiny mouse sets up his home and builds
His granaries, or sightless moles dig out

[1] Demeter.

Their nests: in holes there will you find the toad,
And all the countless pests that Earth engenders;
Or a huge heap of grain weevils will ravage,
And the ant that dreads a destitute old age.
   Mark also, when in orchards many an almond
Puts on her robe of blossom and bends down
Her fragrant branches: if the fruit prevail,
The corn-crops will keep pace, and a great threshing
Will come with a great heat; but if thick shade   190
Abound in leafy luxury, your floor,
Rich only in chaff, shall thresh mere stalks in vain.
I have seen many a sower treat his seeds,
And before sowing drench them first in soda
And black oil-lees, that the deceitful pods
Might yield the larger produce, and the beans
Be quickly sodden, however small the fire.
I have seen how seeds, long picked, and with much pains
Examined, yet degenerate, unless
Year after year human toil has culled out
By hand the largest. Thus all things are fated
To hasten towards the worse, and slipping away   200
Are carried backwards; just as, if some rower
Who scarce can force his boat against the stream,
Should suddenly relax his arms, forthwith
Headlong down the river the current sweeps it.
   Furthermore we must watch the star of Arcturus,
The season of the Kids, and the bright Snake,
As heedfully as they who, voyaging home
O'er windy seas, brave Pontus and the straits
Of oyster-breeding Abydus. When the Scales
Make equal the hours of daytime and of sleep,
And part in twain the circle of the heavens,
Half light, half shade, then manfully work your oxen,   210
And sow your fields with barley, until the coming
Of winter's rains, when none can labour more.
Now is the time for covering in the soil
Your flax seeds, and the poppy Ceres loves;

And now delay no more but bend to the plough,
While the dry soil will let you and the clouds
Still float on high. Spring is the sowing-time
For beans; then too the crumbling furrows welcome
Median clover, and the millet needs
Our yearly care, when white with gilded horns
The Bull opens the year, and the Dog sinks
Confronting still the star that follows him.
But if the crop for which you plough the soil
Be wheat or hardy spelt, and if your aim   220
Be corn alone, let Atlas' daughters[1] first
Hide themselves in the morning from your sight,
And let the Gnosian star of the bright Crown
Withdraw, ere to the furrows you commit
The due seeds, or too hastily entrust
The hope of the year to a reluctant soil.
Many ere Maia's[2] setting have begun
Their sowing, but the looked-for crop has mocked them
With empty ears. Yet if you sow the vetch
Or homely kidney-bean, nor scorn the culture
Of Pelusiac[3] lentils, then no doubtful signs
Will the Herdsman send you as he sets. Begin,
Nor cease your sowing till mid-winter's frost.   230
　　Therefore his annual circuit the golden Sun
Governs and measures out into fixed paths
Through the twelve constellations of the heavens.[4]
Five zones divide the sky; whereof the first
Is ever glowing under the sun's bright rays,
Ever scorched by his fire. Round these, two zones
At the far poles to right and left stretch out
All dark with black storms and congealed with ice.
Between these and the middle zone, are two
Which by the grace of the Gods have been vouchsafed
To frail men, and a path is cut between them
Where the Signs may revolve in slanting order.

[1] The Pleiades.   [2] One of the Pleiades.
[3] Egyptian.   [4] The Signs of the Zodiac.

As above Scythia and the Rhipaean mountains   240
The sphere of heaven rises, so it sinks
And slopes down over Libya's southern clime.
One pole is ever high above our heads;
But the other is beheld beneath our feet
By murky Styx and the deep buried ghosts.
Here in our Northern sphere with sinuous coils
The great Snake like a river glides around
And between the two Bears—the Bears who dread
To plunge neath Ocean's plain: but there, men say,
Is either silence and blank timeless night,
And darkness dense and denser evermore
Beneath the pall of night; or else from us
The dawn returns, and there brings back the day;
And when on us the rising Sun first breathes   250
With panting steeds, there glowing Vesper is kindling
His evening beams. Hence, though the sky be doubtful,
We may foretell the weather's changes; hence
Harvest and sowing time; when first to lash
With oars the treacherous calm, and when to launch
Our well-rigged fleet, or in the woods to fell
The pine in season. Not in vain we watch
The Signs rising and setting, and the year
Evenly balanced by its four diverse seasons.
      Whenever cold rains keep the husbandman
Indoors, he can prepare at leisure much   260
That in fine weather must be done in haste.
The ploughman hammers out the blunted share's
Hard tooth, scoops troughs from trees, or brands the sheep,
Or stamps numbers upon his bins of corn.
Others may sharpen stakes or two-pronged forks,
And for the pliant vine cut withes of willow.
Now of bramble twigs let soft baskets be woven;
Now roast the corn, now grind it with the stone.
Why, even on holy days law, both divine
And human, will permit men to perform
Certain tasks. Never did religious scruple

Forbid us to guide down the rivulets,   270
To fence corn with a hedge, or to set snares
For birds, to fire brambles, or to plunge
The bleating flocks into the health-giving river.
Often too will the farmer load the flanks
Of his slow donkey with cheap fruits or oil,
And when he comes home bring back from the town
A lump of black pitch or a chiseled millstone.

    The Moon has appointed some days in one class,
Some in another, as lucky for our labours.
Avoid the fifth; for on that day were born
Pale Orcus and the Furies; then it was
That with unholy labour Earth engendered
Iapetus and Coëus and the fierce
Typhōeus, and those brethren who conspired   280
To tear down Heaven.[1] Thrice verily did they strive
To heap Ossa on Pelion, and upheave
Leafy Olympus onto Ossa's back;
Thrice did the Father with his thunderbolt
Smite down and scatter apart their piled-up mountains.
For planting vines the seventeenth day is lucky,
Also for taming young steers to the yoke,
And fastening leashes to a loom. The ninth
Is good for runaways but bad for thieving.

    Many tasks are more suitably performed
Either in the cool of night, or when at sunrise
The morning star washes the earth with dew.
By night it's best to cut light straw; by night
To mow dry meadows: softening moisture fails not   290
At night-time. One I know who sits up late
By winter fire-light, and with his sharp knife
Points torches. Meanwhile, solacing with a song
Her tedious toil, his wife shoots through the web
Her tuneful shuttle, or boils down on the fire
The sweet juice of the unfermented wine,

[1] The Giants.

And skims with leaves the simmering cauldron's foam.
But in the heat of noonday should be reaped
The ruddy corn, and on the threshing-floor
In the noon's heat the parched ears should be bruised.
Strip to plough, strip to sow; for husbandmen
Winter is a lazy time. In the cold months
Peasants are wont to enjoy their gains, and love   300
To feast together in convivial jollity.
Genial Winter invites them and dissolves
All thought of care; just as when vessels laden
With merchandise have at last reached their port,
And the glad sailors wreathe the sterns with garlands.
And yet then is the time to gather acorns,
Berries of laurel, olives and blood-red myrtle;
Then is the time to set springes for cranes,
And nets for stags, and chase the long-eared hares,
To strike the does whirling the hempen sling,
When snow lies deep, when rivers pack their ice.   310
    Of Autumn's fitful weather and its stars
Why tell? and what the dangers husbandmen
Must watch for, as now shorter grows the day,
Milder the summer's heat, or else when spring
Pours down in rain-showers, when with ears of corn
Already the land is bristling, and the grain
On its green stalk with milky juice is swelling.
Often have I beheld how, when the farmer
Has brought the reapers into his yellow fields,
And is now stripping from their brittle stalks
The barley ears—how all the battling winds
Together rushing tear up roots and all
The ripe corn far and wide, and high in the air
Scatter it; till light stalks and flying stubble   320
The storm with its black whirlwind sweeps away.
Often too, marching across the sky there comes
A mighty host of waters, and the clouds,
Mustering from the sea, are massed together
Into a dreadful tempest of black rains.

The whole sky falls, and with one vast downpour
Washes away the flourishing crops and all
The labours of the oxen. The dykes fill;
The streams in their deep channels swell and roar,
And the sea boils within its panting firths.
The Sky-god from amid that night of clouds
Hurls forth his thunder from a flashing hand.
At the shock trembles the wide earth; to shelter
Straightway the beasts flee, and throughout whole nations 330
Cowering fear lays prostrate mortal hearts,
As with his fiery thunderbolt he strikes
Athos or Rhodope or Ceraunia's crests.
The winds redouble; heavily falls the rain;
Now woods, now shores wail in that mighty blast.
   In dread of such disaster, note the months
And planets; whither Saturn's chilly star
Withdraws; into what regions of the sky
Strays the Cyllenian fire.[1] But above all
Worship the Gods, and pay her yearly rites
To the Corn-goddess, offering sacrifice
Upon the young grass, when at last the winter
Is over and gone, and spring makes bright the sky.   340
Then lambs are fat, and wines are then most mellow;
Sleep then is sweet, and shade thick on the hills.
Let all your rustic youth now worship Ceres:
For her in milk and soft wine you must drench
The honeycomb, and the auspicious victim
Must be led three times round the growing crops,
Followed by the whole chorus of your fellows
With loud exulting cries summoning Ceres
To dwell within their homes. And let none put
His sickle to the ripe corn, till, his brows
With oak-wreath crowned, he has flung artless gambols
And sung his harvest hymns in Ceres' honour.   350
   And that by sure signs we may learn these dangers,

[1] The planet Mercury.

Both heats and rains and winds that bring cold weather,
The Father has himself ordained what warnings
The monthly moon should give, what signs foretell
The falling of the wind, what well-known sights
Should warn the farmer he must keep his cattle
Close to their stalls. Thus, when the winds are rising,
First will the sea begin to heave and swell,
And dry cracklings are heard on the high mountains;
Then from the shore echoing afar there comes
A confused noise, and in the woods the roar
Grows louder. Now already the waves are threatening　360
The curved ships; gulls fly swiftly from mid-sea
And alight screaming on the shore; the coot
Sports on dry land; leaving its marshy haunts
The heron soars aloft above the clouds.
Often again, when wind is threatening,
You will see stars glide swiftly down the sky
Leaving behind them long white trails of fire
Against night's darkness: often will light chaff
And fallen leaves be blown about, or feathers
Dance together over the water's surface.
But when from the grim regions of the North　　　370
It lightens, when the quarters of the East
Or West are thundering, then with flooded ditches
All the fields are aswim, and out at sea
Every mariner furls his dripping sails.
Never has rain brought injury to men
At unawares; for either, as it is gathering,
Cranes will have fled before it from on high
To the deep valleys; or else gazing skyward
The steer with open nostril snuffs the breeze,
Or twittering swallows flit around the lakes,
While in the mud frogs croak their ancient plaint.
And oftentimes, wearing a narrow path,
Out of her secret galleries the ant
Bears forth her eggs; and the great rainbow drinks:　380
Legions of rooks quitting their feeding-ground

In one vast host clamour with serried wings.
Also the various sea-birds, and all those
That love Cayster's[1] pools, and roam exploring
The Asian meadow-lands, you then may see
In playful rivalry pouring showers of spray
Over their backs, now plunging into the waters
Head-foremost, now racing to meet the waves
Exulting in the bath with aimless rapture.
Then the malignant raven with deep croak
Summons the rain, as by itself alone
It stalks on the dry sand. Even at night
Maidens, spinning their tasks, become aware   390
That a storm is approaching, when they see
How the oil splutters in the flaming lamp
And stinking snuff is gathering on the wick.

   After wet weather no less easily
May you foresee bright suns and cloudless skies,
And know them by clear signs; for then unblurred
Will appear the sharp edges of the stars,
While under no debt to her brother's rays
The moon will rise,[2] and no thin fleecy clouds
Will drift across the blue; nor do the Halcyons,
Beloved by Thetis, spread their wings on the shore
In the warm sun; nor do uncleanly swine
Delight in tossing to pieces with their snouts   400
Their straw bedding. Rather do clouds hang low,
And rest upon the plain; and as she watches
The sunset, perched on some tall tree, the owl
Utters her strident evening call in vain.
High up in the clear lift Nisus appears,
While Scylla[3] for that purple lock she stole

---

[1] A river in Lydia.
[2] Perhaps this means that the moon is so brilliant that it *appears* to shine with its own light.
[3] Scylla, daughter of Nisus, king of Megara, falling in love with his enemy, Minos, cut from her father's head the 'purple lock' on which his life depended. The gods changed Scylla into a sea-bird, and Nisus into an osprey.

Must suffer vengeance. Wherever in her flight
She cleaves the light air with her wings, lo there,
Relentless, savage, Nisus with loud whirr
Pursues her through the sky; wherever Nisus
Soars skyward, there, fleeing from his pursuit,
Swiftly she cleaves the light air with her wings.
Then softly cawing do the rooks repeat   410
Thrice or four times clear mellow croaks, and often
In their high nests gladdened beyond their wont
By some mysterious sweetness, among the leaves
Chatter together. Joy it is to them,
Now that the rains are over, to return
Home to their little brood and beloved nests;
Not, I believe, that Heaven has given them
Intelligence, or Fate a larger foresight
Of things to come; but that now, when the weather
And fitful vapours of the sky have changed,
When wet with southern gales the Sky-god thickens
What of late was rare, then dissolves what was dense,
The phases of their minds then change, their hearts   420
Feel other motions now than when the wind
Was driving along the clouds. Hence in the fields
Those quires of birds are chanting, beasts for joy
Leaping, and rooks cawing in exultation.

  But if you pay heed to the fiery sun
And to the sequent phases of the moon,
The morrow will never play you false, nor yet
Will you be cheated by a cloudless night.
If, when the new moon is regathering
Her brightness, she embrace within dim horns
A dark air, then will heavy rain betide
Farmers and seamen. But if she suffuse   430
Her face with virgin blushes, there'll be wind.
When there's wind, golden Phoebe ever blushes.
But if on her fourth rising (and this sign
Will not deceive us) she float through the sky
Clear and with horns unblurred, then all that day,

And all the days that follow to the month's end,
Will be unvexed by wind or rain; and sailors
For a safe landing will fulfil on shore
Their vows to Glaucus and to Panopēa
Or to the child of Ino, Melicertes.
   Also the Sun, alike when he is rising
And sinking under the waves, will give you signs:
No signs are surer than the sun's, both those
He brings each morning, and when the stars are rising.   440
If, buried within cloud, he has flecked with spots
His early dawn, and to his central disk
Has shrunk back, then you must beware of showers;
For from the sea is driving a south wind
That bodes no good to trees and crops and cattle.
And when at daybreak spreading shafts of light
Break out between thick cloud; or when Aurora
Rises pale from Tithonus' saffron bed,
Alas, then vainly will the vine-leaf shelter
Your ripening grapes; such pelting multitudes
Of hailstones will dance rattling on the roofs.
This warning it will even more profit you   450
To bear in mind: when, after traversing
The sky, he is now departing, we often see
Various colours fluctuate on his face.
A dark hue portends rain, a flame-like glow
East winds; but if dark spots and ruddy fire
Begin to blend, soon will you see the sky
Mingled in one turmoil of wind and storm-clouds.
On such a night let no one counsel me
To unmoor from land and launch out on the deep.
But if, both when he brings back day and buries
The day he brought, his orb be bright, then vain
Will be your fear of clouds, and you may watch
The forests waving in a clear north wind.   460
   Finally, what late evening has in store,
The quarter whence the breeze will drive bright clouds
Before it, what the moist south wind is brooding,

The Sun will give you signs. And who shall dare
Call the Sun false? Nay, he will often warn us
Of rebellions that lurk and threaten, of treachery,
And of the hidden cancerous growth of wars.
He too, when Caesar died, had pity on Rome,
And muffled up the brightness of his head
In lurid gloom, so that a godless age
Dreaded eternal night; though at that time
Earth also and the waters of the sea
And unclean dogs and birds of evil omen   470
Warned us of doom to come. How often saw we
Aetna forth from her bursting furnaces
With fiery rivers flood the fields of Sicily,
Vomiting balls of fire and molten rocks!
Arms clashing in the sky Germania heard,
And with unwonted shuddering the Alps quaked.
A voice too mid the silence of sacred groves
Was heard of many—a mighty voice; and phantoms,
Pale in wondrous wise, were seen when night
Grew dim; and cattle spoke, a fearful portent!
Rivers stop flowing; earth gapes wide; in temples
Ivory weeps in sorrow, and bronzes sweat.   480
Eridanus,[1] king of rivers, washed away
Whole forests in his raging swirl, and swept along
Herds and their stalls together throughout the plain.
Nor at that time did the priest fail to find
Threatening filaments in ill-omened victims:
Blood too would ooze in wells, and high-built towns
Would echo nightlong with the howl of wolves.
Never did baleful comets blaze so often;
Never from cloudless skies more lightnings fell.
Therefore a second time Philippi saw
Romans meeting in battle armed alike;   490
Nor did the Gods deem it shameful that twice
Emathia should be fattened with our blood,
And the wide plains of Haemus.[2] Verily a time

[1] The Po.   [2] An allusion to the battles of Pharsalia and Philippi.

Will come when in those fields the husbandman,
Labouring the earth with his curved plough, shall find
Pilums eaten away with scaly rust,
Or strike on empty helms with heavy hoe,
And marvel at giant bones dug from their graves.

Gods of our country, Heroes of her soil,
Yea thou, Romulus, and thou Mother Vesta,
Guardian of Tuscan Tiber and Roman Palatine,
At least forbid not this young prince[1] to succour   500
Our ruined age. Long enough has our blood
Paid for Laomedon's perjury at Troy;[2]
Long enough, Caesar, have the courts of Heaven
Grudged us your presence here on earth, complaining
That you seek mortal triumphs only, here
Where right with wrong, wrong with right is confounded;
Where with so many wars this world is troubled,
So many shapes of sin; where to the plough
Due honour is no more paid: reft of its labourers
Our tilth must lie forlorn, and our curved sickles
Be melted down and forged into strong sword-blades.
Here the Euphrates, there Germania wakens war:
Neighbouring cities break the leagues that bound them   510
And arm themselves in haste; through the whole world
Rages the God of impious civil strife.
So racing chariots bursting from their stalls
Gather speed lap by lap; the charioteer,
Tugging at the bit in vain, is swept along
By his horses, and the car heeds not the reins.

[1] Caesar Augustus.
[2] Apollo and Poseidon built the walls of Troy for King Laomedon, who then refused them their promised wages. His perjury brought a perpetual curse on the Trojan race, and so, through Aeneas, on the Romans.

THE GEORGICS

BOOK TWO

Thus far the tilth of fields and stars of heaven;
Now will I sing thee, Bacchus, and with thee
The saplings of the woodlands, and the fruit
Of the slow-growing olive. Hither come,
Lord of the wine-press; for here all is full
Of thy good gifts: for thee the field is gay
Laden with vine-dressed autumn, and the vintage
Foams in the brimming vats. Come hither then,
Lord of the wine-press, doff your buskins, and with me
In the new must dye purple your bare legs.
    First of all, diverse is the nature of trees
Whereby they are born and grow. For some, by man   10
Unplanted, of their own free will spring up,
And over plains and along winding rivers
Spread far and wide. Such are the soft osier,
The lithe shoots of the broom, the poplar tree,
And whitening willow-beds with grey-green leafage.
But some spring from dropped seed, as tall chestnuts,
And that tree, mightiest of the woods, that spreads
Its foliage in Jove's honour, and those oaks
Deemed by the Greeks oracular. With others,
Such as the elm and cherry, a dense undergrowth
Springs from their roots; and the Parnassian bay-tree
Beneath its mother's vast shade pushes up
A tiny shoot. These modes did Nature first   20
Ordain; these give their verdure to every kind
Of forest-tree and shrub and sacred grove.
    Other modes are there which experience
From time to time has found out of itself.
Some from the mother's tender frame tear suckers

And plant them out in furrows; another buries
Stems in the ground, whether as cross-cleft shafts
Or as sharp-pointed stakes. Some trees await
The layer's bent-down arch, and quickset slips
In their own soil. Other kinds need no root,
And so the pruner fears not to restore
The topmost twig to the earth. Nay, when the trunk
Has been sawed through (marvellous to relate),   30
From the dry log an olive root thrusts forth.
And oft we see how one tree's branches change
Into another's without injury,
So that the pear, transformed, bears grafted apples,
And stony cornels redden on the plum.
   Come then, husbandmen, learn the training proper
To each tree in its kind; tame your wild fruits
By cultivation, and suffer not your land
To lie idle. What joy it were to plant
All Ismarus[1] with the vine, and clothe with olive
Mighty Taburnus! And do thou aid me now,
Maecenas, thou my glory, and by just due   40
Chief sharer of my fame; speed thou with me
Upon this toilsome voyage I have begun,
And spread thy swift sails over a spacious sea.
I seek not in my verses to embrace
This whole theme, not though mine were a hundred tongues,
A hundred mouths, a voice of iron. Yet aid me,
And skirt the coastline: near will be the land.
In wandering mazes here will I not detain you
With mythic strains and preludes long drawn out.
   Those trees that into the borders of the light
Rise of their own free will, spring up unfruitful
But strong and flourishing; for beneath the soil
There lurks creative power. Yet even these,
If you should graft them, or, when so transformed,   50
Plant them in well-worked trenches, will put off

[1] A mountain in Thrace. Taburnus was near Naples.

Their wild-wood nature, and under constant tillage
Soon learn what lesson you may choose to teach them.
Even that shoot which springs, a barren sucker,
From the tree's foot, would become no less fertile
If planted out in open ground; but now
The mother-tree, o'ershadowing its growth
With deep-foliaged boughs, robs it of produce,
Withering up its efforts to bear fruit.
Lastly the tree that rises from dropped seed
Comes up slowly, and will yield its shade
To our children's children: its fruits too degenerate,
Forgetting their old savour, and the vine
Bears starveling clusters for the birds to pillage.   60

On all in truth must we spend labour; all
Must be forced into furrows and there tamed,
Cost what it may. But olives answer best
From truncheons, vines from layers, Paphian myrtles
From solid stems: from slips are hardy hazels
Born, and the huge ash, and that shady tree
That gave his wreath to Hercules,[1] and the oak
Of the Chaonian Sire: thus too are born
The tall palm, and the fir that must behold
The perils of the sea. But 'tis by grafting
That on the rough-barked arbute walnuts ripen,
And sterile planes bear thriving apple boughs: 70
With snowy chestnut flowers the beech grows white,
The ash tree with pear blossom, and swine crunch
Acorns that they have found beneath the elm.

Nor are the modes of budding and of grafting
One and the same; for where the buds push out
From under the bark, and burst their delicate sheaths,
A narrow slit is made just on the knot;
In this they insert a bud from an alien tree,
And teach it to grow into the sappy rind.
Or else boles that are knotless are cut back,

[1] The poplar.

And a way is cleft by wedges deep within
The solid wood; then the fruit-bearing slips
Are thrust in; and before long a huge tree   80
Shoots heavenward with fertile branches, marvelling
At its strange leafage and fruits not its own.
   Furthermore of one single kind are neither
Stalwart elms, nor the willow and lotus-tree,
Nor cypresses of Ida; and fat olives
Are of quite different types: there is the orchad,
The radius, and the bitter-berried pausian.
Apples too, and the fruit-trees of Alcinous
Vary in kind; nor from the same scion
Do Syrian and Crustumian pears grow,
Or heavy wardens. So the vintages
That hang from our own trees are not the same
As Lesbos gathers from Methymne's sprays.   90
Thasian and white Mareotic vines there are,
These suited for rich soils, for lighter those;
The Psithian too, useful for raisin-wine,
And that subtle Lagean which some day
Is sure to trouble the feet and tie the tongue;
The Purple and the Precian; and thou, Rhaetic,
How shall I sing thy praises? Yet even so
Vie not, I warn thee, with Falernian cellars.
Likewise there are Picenian vines that give
The soundest wine of all, to which the Tmolian
And even the royal Chian must pay homage;
Also the lesser Argītis, which no wine
May rival, whether in abundant yield,   100
Or in lasting through long years. Thee, vine of Rhodes,
Let me not pass by, welcome to the Gods
And to the banquet's second course; nor thee,
Bumastus, with thy swelling grape-clusters.
But how many kinds there are, and what their names,
Vain would it be to reckon; nor indeed
Would reckoning be worth while. He who should wish
For such knowledge, would likewise wish to learn

How many grains of sand on Libya's plain
Are stirred by the west wind; or when the East
Falls with unwonted violence on the ships,
Would wish to know how many were the waves
That across the Ionian sea come rolling shoreward.

By no means can all soils give birth to all things.
By rivers willows grow, in swampy fens   110
Alders, on stony hills the barren ash;
On sea-shores myrtle bushes thrive most happily;
While open sunny slopes the Wine-god loves,
Yew trees the north wind and the cold. See too
How the earth's most distant lands by man's tillage
Have been subdued; how in the East dwell Arabs,
Painted Gelonians in the North: no less
Various are the native climes of trees.
Alone India bears black ebony;
Alone to the Sabaeans does the branch
Of frankincense belong. Why should I tell you
Of the balsams that drip from fragrant wood,
Or of the berries of evergreen acanthus?
Why tell of Ethiopian shrubs that whiten   120
With downy wool,[1] or how the Chinese comb
Their fine fleeces from leaves?[2] or of the forests
Which India rears, that land at the world's end
Hard by the Ocean, where no arrow's flight
Can oversoar those heaven-towering trees?
Yet not slow is that race in feats of archery.
Media bears the sour-juiced clinging savour
Of the health-giving citron, than which naught
Comes as a help more sovereign to drive out
The deadly poison from the limbs, if haply
Some murderous stepdame shall have drugged the cup
Mingling within it herbs and baleful charms.   130
This tree is large, in aspect like a bay;
And but for the different scent it flings abroad,

---

[1] I.e. cotton.   [2] Silk was then supposed to grow on trees.

A bay indeed it were. The leaves fall not
In any wind; no flowers cling more closely.
The Medes use it for rinsing a foul-breathed mouth,
And as a cure for asthma in old men.
   But neither Media's wealth of citron groves,
Nor fair Ganges, nor Hermus rolling down
His golden silt, may vie with Italy's glory—
Not Bactra, no nor India, nor all Panchaia
So rich in spicy sands. This soil no bulls   140
With nostrils breathing fire have ever ploughed
For the sowing of a monstrous dragon's teeth;
No crop of men has bristled here with helms
And serried lances; but with teeming corn
This land is filled, and with the juice of Bacchus;
A land of olives and of prosperous cattle.
Hers is the war-horse, pacing proudly o'er the plain;
Hers too, Clitumnus,[1] are thy snow-white herds
Which, with the bull, noblest among victims,
Bathed in thy sacred stream, have oft-times led
Rome's triumphs to the temples of her Gods.
Here is abiding spring, and summer lingering
Into months not her own: twice in one year
Breed cattle, twice the fruit-tree yields its produce.   150
But ravening tigers and the savage brood
Of lions there are none: monkshood deludes not
The wretch who plucks it; nor does the scaly serpent,
Darting his monstrous coils along the ground,
Gather so vast a length into a spire.
Then call to mind so many glorious cities
Built by man's skill and toil, so many towns
Reared by his labour on precipitous crags,
And rivers gliding beneath ancient walls.
Of her seas shall I tell, that wash her shores
From above, from below? of her great lakes?
Of thee the greatest, Larius,[2] and of thee,
Benacus, surging with the swell and roar   160

[1] A river in Umbria.   [2] Larius is Lake Como, Benacus is Lake Garda.

Of ocean? Of her harbours shall I tell,
And of the barrier set upon the Lucrine,[1]
And the loud thunders of the indignant sea,
While far away are heard the Julian waves
Broken and flung back, as the Tyrrhene tide
Pours foaming into the channels of Avernus?
This land moreover has mines that reveal
Rivers of silver and copper in rich veins,
And abundant streams of gold: and she has reared
A valiant race of men, the Marsians,
The Sabine stock, the Ligurian inured
To hardship, and the javelin-bearing Volscian:
She has reared the Decii and the Marii too,
And great Camillus, the two Scipios
Stubborn in battle, and thee, greatest Caesar,   170
Who in our days, a conqueror even now
In Asia's farthest bounds, art driving back
The unwarlike Indians[2] from the towers of Rome.
Hail, thou land of Saturn, mighty mother
Of harvests, mighty mother of brave men!
For thee am I now entering on this theme
Of the glories and skill of ancient days;
For thee I dare to unseal the sacred founts,
And sing through Roman towns a song of Ascra.[3]

We come now to the temper of each field,
Their strength, their colour, and their native power
Of bearing produce. First then churlish soils
And niggard hillsides, where there is lean clay,   180
And brambly stone-strewn acres; these delight
In long-lived olive groves that Pallas loves:
In sign whereof on the same land springs up
Many an oleaster, and the ground
Is strewed with its wild berries. But a fat loam

[1] The Lucrine and Avernian were two small lakes close to the Bay of Naples.
[2] By Indians he means Orientals in general.
[3] Hesiod, author of *Works and Days*, was born at Ascra in Boeotia.

Rejoicing in fresh moisture, a plain thick
With herbage and of rich fertility
(Such we may often see in a hollow vale
Within some mountain, from whose rocky heights
Streams trickle down fraught with prolific mud),
A land that faces south and feeds the fern
So hateful to the plough—this land some day
Will yield you hardy vines, whence you may press   190
A bounteous vintage—yield you grapes in plenty,
And such juice as from golden bowls we pour,
When by the altars the fat-bellied Tuscan
Has blown his ivory pipe, and in broad chargers
We offer steaming entrails to the Gods.

   But if your wish be rather to keep cattle,
And calves or lambs, or kids that blight young plants,
Then journey to the distant glades and meadows
Of rich Tarentum, or to such a plain
As hapless Mantua lost, where snow-white swans
Feed in the weedy river. There your flocks
Will lack neither clear springs nor pasturage;   200
And all that in the long days your herds crop,
The cool dew of a brief night will restore.

   Land that is black, revealing a rich loam
Under the share's pressure, and with a soil
That crumbles (this it is we imitate
By ploughing), is in general best for corn.
There is no other land whence you may see
More wagons wending home behind slow oxen.
That soil is good too, whence the impatient husbandman
Has carted away the forest-trees, and felled
The woods that have stood idle many a year,
Tearing up, roots and all, those ancient haunts
Where the birds nested. From their abandoned homes   210
Into the sky they are flown. The land that once
Lay wild, now gleams under the driven ploughshare.
As for the hungry gravel of the hills,
It scarce can serve the bees with lowly spurge

And rosemary; while rough tufa, and the chalk
Tunnelled by snakes, boast that no other fields
Can so well supply serpents with the food
They love, or furnish them with winding holes.
Land that exhales thin mist and flitting vapours,
And drinks in moisture and throws it off at will,
That always robes itself in its own green
Mantle of grass, that does not corrode steel   220
With a salt scurf of rust—that land will garland
Your elms with joyous vines; will yield you oil
In plenty; and when you've tilled it, will prove kindly
To cattle, and submit to the curved share.
Such is the soil rich Capua ploughs, and such the coast
That neighbours the Vesuvian mount, and Clanius
Whose floods are cruel to desolate Acerrae.
    Now will I tell you how you may distinguish
The qualities of each soil. If you would know
Whether it be loose or stiff beyond the wont
(For the one is good for corn, for vines the other;
The stiffer land for Ceres, all loose soils
For Bacchus), you must first look out a place,   230
Then bid a pit be sunk deep in the ground,
And into this put all the earth back and stamp
The surface level. If there is not enough
To fill the hole up, that soil will be loose,
Fitter for cattle and for generous vines.
But if the earth refuses to return
To its old place, and there is some left over
After the pit is filled, that soil is dense:
Look for reluctant clods and clotted ridges:
To plough such ground you will need sturdy heifers.
As for a salty land, the kind called sour
(Unfruitful it is for corn, nor is it mellowed
By ploughing: it preserves not for the vine
Its lineage, nor for orchard-fruits their fame),   240
Thus you may test it: from your smoky roof
Pull down your baskets of close-plaited osiers,

Through which you strain your wine, and into these
Let that bad soil mixed with fresh spring-water
Be pressed in to the brim: then all the moisture
Will be squeezed out, and you will see large drops
Trickling between the wythies; but the taste
Will tell a plain tale, and with its sour flavour
Will wrinkle awry the face of those who try it.
Also whether the soil be rich we learn
In this way best: never, when with your hands
You work it, does it crumble, but like pitch
Grows sticky on the fingers as you handle it.   250
Moist soil nurtures tall grass: its natural growth
Is ranker than it should be. Ah, not thus
Over-fertile let *my* soil be, nor ever
Show itself too strong when the ears first form!
Silently, by mere weight a heavy soil
Betrays itself; so does a light one too.
At a first glance the eye will know black soil,
And which land has which colour. But to detect
A villainous cold ground is difficult;
Only pitch-pines and poisonous yew trees
Or dark ivy sometimes reveal its traces.
    When to these precepts you have given good heed,
First, long before you plant the vine's glad stock,
Remember to sun-bake the land, and trenching   260
Its broad hillsides, expose to the north wind
Its upturned clods. Those fields are best that have
A crumbling soil. The winds will see to this,
And the cold frosts, and the stout delver too,
Whose spade breaks up and loosens the whole ground.
But men whose vigilant care nothing escapes,
Seek beforehand the place where the young vines
May be got ready for the supporting trees,
A place like that to which they may be carried
When planted out, lest through the sudden change
The nurslings should feel strangely to their mother.
What's more, they print the quarter of the heavens

Upon the bark, so that they may replace,
As each stood first, the side whereon it bore 270
The southern heats, the back it turned to the north:
So strong are habits formed in tender age.

Enquire beforehand whether it be better
To plant the vine on hilly or level ground.
If 'tis a rich plain you are laying out,
Plant close: in soil close-planted the Wine-god
Is none the less prolific. But if it be
A soil of rising knolls and sloping hills,
Give your rows room. None the less, when you have planted
Your trees, let every avenue, wherever
It intersects a cross-path, square to a nicety.
As often in mighty warfare when the legion
Has deployed all its cohorts in long line,
And on the open plain the column halts, 280
When the ranks are drawn out, and all the land
Far and wide ripples with the gleam of brass,
Nor yet has the grim fray been joined, but doubtfully
Between the armoured hosts the War-god hovers—
Just so must all be spaced in regular paths
Symmetrically, not merely that the view
May feed an idle fancy, but because
In that way only may the earth afford
An equal strength to all, and so allow
The branches to spread forth into empty air.

If you should ask how deep must be the trenches—
The vine with confidence would I entrust
To a shallow furrow; the supporting tree
Must be sunk deeper and far within the earth; 290
Above all the great oak, which with her roots
Strikes downward towards Tartarus as far
As to the airs of heaven she lifts her summit.
Her therefore neither winter storms, nor blasts,
Nor rains may uproot, but unmoved she abides,
And many generations, many ages
Of mortals she outlives, while they roll by

And she endures. Her stalwart boughs like arms
She stretches out on every side, herself
The centre, still upholding a mighty shade.

    Let not your vineyard slope towards the sunset;
Nor plant the hazel among your vines; nor choose
The topmost vine-sprays; nor should you lop off   300
Your cuttings from the tops of trees (so strong
Their love for the earth);[1] nor with a blunted knife
Injure young shoots; neither plant in their midst
Wild trunks of olive. For often careless shepherds
Will drop a spark, which lurking at first unseen
Under the thick bark, fastens on the wood,
And darting out among the leaves above
Sends skyward a huge roar; then, running on
Among the branches and the topmost twigs,
Reigns there victorious, wrapping the whole plantation
In flames, which, thickening to a pitchy darkness,
Pour black clouds up to the heavens—worst of all
If a storm has swooped down upon the trees,   310
And the wind herds and drives the flames before it.
Should this befall, there will be no strength left
Within the vine-stocks, nor when cut away
Can they revive and grow green as before
Out of the deep soil: alone there survives
The barren oleaster with its bitter leaves.

    Let no one, howsoever wise he seem,
Prevail with you to meddle with the soil
While it lies stiff under the north wind's breath.
Then winter seals the land with frost, and when
The shoot is planted, suffers it not to fasten
Its frozen roots in the earth. The best season
For planting vines is when in blushing spring
The white bird[2] comes, that enemy to long snakes;   320
Or else close on the first cold days of autumn,

---

[1] I.e. 'So great is their love for the earth that when they are far
from it they are less vigorous.' Paley.
[2] The white stork.

Before the steeds of the fierce sun have reached
The winter Signs, when summer now is waning.
   Spring it is, spring that aids the woodland leaf
And growing tree; in spring earth swells and yearns
For fertilizing seed. Then it is that Heaven,
The Father omnipotent, in pregnant showers
Descends into the lap of his glad spouse,
And mightily mingling with her mighty body
Nourishes every growth. Then pathless copses
Resound with songs of birds, and then returns
The season when the herds renew their loves;
The teeming land breaks into birth, the fields   330
Loosen their bosoms to the warm zephyr's breath;
A gentle moisture everywhere abounds;
As new suns dawn, the grasses dare encounter them
In safety; the young vine-shoots have no fear
Of rising south winds, or that the mighty North
Will sweep in rain-storms from the sky, but thrust
Every bud forth and unfold all their leaves.
Such, I would fain imagine, were the days
That shone upon the birth of the young world;
Such was creation's dawn. Springtime it was;
Spring was the season the great globe was keeping,
And the east winds forbore their wintry blast,
When the first herds and flocks drank in the light,   340
And the iron race of men reared up its head
From the hard fields, and wild beasts issued forth
Into the woods, and stars into the sky.
Nor would such tender things have strength to endure
This world's hardship, did not so long a respite
Divide the cold months from the hot, and were not
Earth comforted by an indulgent heaven.
   For the rest, whatever young shoots you may plant
About your fields, sprinkle them with rich dung,
And cover them heedfully with soil in plenty;
Or dig in porous pebbles or rough shells;
For then between them water will soak down,

And searching breaths of air will find their way;
Whence the plants will take courage. We have known 350
Of farmers who would place a stone above them,
Or a great heavy potsherd, as a shield
Against rain-storms, or when the sultry Dog-star
Cracks the fields until they gape for thirst.

   The shoots once planted, there remains the task
Of breaking up the ground time after time
About the roots, heaving the massive hoe;
Or you must work the soil beneath the plough,
And wheel your straining oxen to and fro
Between the vineyard rows. Make ready then
Smooth reeds, rods of peeled wood, and ashen stakes,
And sturdy forks, by whose support the vines   360
May learn to climb and scorn the wind and run
From tier to tier high up into the elms.

   While they are in their first growth and their leaves
Are new-born, you must spare their tender youth:
And even when the vine-shoot pushes joyously
Towards the sky, racing with loosened rein
Through empty air, you must not yet essay
To prune the plants themselves with the knife's edge,
But with bent fingers should the leaves be plucked
And picked off here and there. Later, when now
They have shot up, and with their lusty stems
Embraced the elms, then strip their leaves; then lop
Their branching arms (till now they have feared the knife);
Then at last must your discipline be stern,
And check the luxury of the flowing bough.   370

   Also you must weave hedges and keep out
All cattle, chiefly while the leaf is tender
And ignorant yet of trouble; since beside
Harsh winters and the tyrant sun, wild buffaloes
And pestering roes are ever preying on it,
While sheep and greedy steers make it their pasture.
No cold, stiff with white frost, no summer heat
Heavily brooding over the parched rocks

Can do the vines such injury as the sheep
With their sharp poisonous teeth, indenting scars
Upon the gnawed stem. For no crime but this   380
At every altar a goat is slain to Bacchus,
When the antique plays advance upon the stage;
For the Athenians in their villages
And at their cross-road gatherings ordained
Prizes for wit, and in their drunken jollity
Danced on oiled goat-skins over the grassy meadows.
Likewise the Ausonian[1] peasantry, a race
Migrant from Troy, make merry with uncouth verses
And riotous laughter, wearing frightful masks
Of hollowed bark, and upon thee, Bacchus,
In rollicking songs they call, to thee hang up
Soft waxen faces on the lofty pine.
Thus with rich clusters every vineyard ripens;   390
Fruitful will be all valleys and deep glens
Whereto the God has turned his comely face.
Duly then in the songs our fathers sung
To Bacchus will we chant the praise we owe him,
Offering cakes and dishes: led by the horn
The sacred goat shall stand beside the altar,
And the fat flesh we'll roast on spits of hazel.

   In dressing vines this further task there is,
Whereon never enough pains can be spent:
Thrice or four times each year must all your soil
Be ploughed up, and the clods with the hoe's back
Ceaselessly broken; and the whole plantation   400
Has to be lightened of its foliage.
For husbandmen their toil comes circling back,
Even as the year rolls round into itself
Over its own footprints. And so already,
Soon as the vines have shed their lingering leaves,
And chill winds from the north have shaken down
Their glory from the woods, already now
The industrious farmer's careful thought will reach

[1] I.e. Italian.

Into the coming year: with the curved hook
Of Saturn he attacks the vine he had left,
Clipping it round and shaping it by pruning.
See that you be the first to dig the ground,
The first to cart away and burn the prunings,
The first to carry the poles indoors; the last
To cull your harvest. Twice the vines with shade   410
Are darkened; twice will weeds and thronging briars
Cover the ground: heavy is either task.
Praise large estates, but cultivate a small one.
Then in the woods rough shoots of butcher's broom
Are cut, and rushes on the river-bank;[1]
And the wild willow-bed will keep you at work.
Now are the vines tied up, now the plantations
Discard the knife, now the last vine-dresser
Sings over his finished rows; yet must you still
Keep the soil busy, and stir the dust, and dread
For your now ripened grapes the Sky-god's rage.

But olives need no culture: *they* look not   420
For the curved hook or tearing hoe, when once
They have struck root in the fields and braved the winds.
Earth itself, when the crooked fang unlocks it,
Will yield moisture enough, and heavy corn-crops
If you have ploughed it well. After this mode
Nurture the plump olive, so dear to Peace.

Fruit-trees likewise, so soon as they have felt
Strength in their trunks, and come to their full vigour,
With native force push skyward rapidly
Needing no help from us. No less meanwhile
The woodlands teem with fruit, and with blood-red
Berries the wild haunts of the birds are blushing.   430
Cattle browse on the cytisus, tall forests
Yield pine-torches, and nightly fires are fed
And pour forth light. And can men hesitate
To plant and lavish care? Why should I tell
Of larger trees? Willows and lowly broom,

[1] For tying up the vines.

Even these give leaves for sheep and shade for shepherds,
A hedge for crops and pasturage for honey.
What joy it were to gaze upon Cytorus
Waving with box, and those Narycian woods
Of pitch-pine!—to see fields that owe no debt
To the harrow, none to the industry of men!
Even those barren forests on the heights   440
Of Caucasus, which angry eastern blasts
Are ever tearing and tossing, yield some produce,
Each tree after its kind; pines useful timber
For ships, cedars and cypresses for houses.
From such trees husbandmen turn spokes for wheels,
Or shape drums for their wagons, and from such
Men lay curved keels for boats. Withies grow thick
On willows, leaves on elms; but strong spear-shafts
On myrtle and on the cornel trusty in battle;
While yews are bent into Ituraean bows.
So too smooth limes and the lathe-polished box
Take shape, and by sharp steel are hollowed out;   450
So too, sped down the Po, the light alder
Swims on the raging waves; and so bees hive
Their swarms in hollow cork-trees, or in the belly
Of a rotting ilex. What gifts of such note
Has Bacchus in his bounty bestowed on us?
Nay, Bacchus even has been the cause of crime.
He it was quelled in death the maddened Centaurs,
Their Rhoetus and their Pholus, and Hylaeus
Menacing the Lapiths with that mighty bowl.

  O husbandmen too fortunate, could they come
To know their own felicity! For whom,
Far from war's discord, Earth, that gives to all
Their just due, lavishes from her soil unbidden   460
An easy sustenance. What though for them
No stately mansion with proud gates disgorges
From all its halls and chambers a huge tide
Of morning clients; nor yet do they gape
At doors inlaid with lovely tortoise-shell,

Or at gold-tricked embroideries, or bronzes
Of Ephyra; though their white wool be not stained
With oriental dye, nor is the service
Of their pure oil tainted by bark of cassia!
Nevertheless theirs is tranquillity
Without care, and a life that knows not fraud,
With store of manifold riches; theirs the peace
Of broad domains, caverns and living lakes;
Deep shady vales, and kine lowing, and soft
Slumbers beneath the trees, all these they know: 470
There are the woodland glades where wild beasts haunt,
Youth patient of toil, inured to penury,
Deities revered and old age reverenced.
Among these folk did Justice leave her last
Footprints as she was passing from the earth.
   But me, first above all, may the sweet Muses,
Whose rites I bear, smitten by a mighty love—
May they receive me as their own, and teach me
The pathways of the heavens and the stars,
The various obscurations of the sun,
And the moon's travails; what may be the cause
Of the earth's quakings; by what force the seas
Swell high, bursting their barriers, and again   480
Sink back into themselves; why winter suns
Are in such haste to dip beneath the ocean,
Or what hindrance holds back the lingering nights.
But if about my heart the blood grown chill
Forbids me to explore those realms of nature,
Then let the country, and the streams that flow
Freshening the vales, content me; may I love
Rivers and woods ingloriously. Oh where
Are those plains! where Spercheüs, and the heights
Where revelling Laconian maidens roam,
Taÿgetus! Oh for one to set me down
In the cool glens of Haemus, there to rest
Sheltered beneath the mighty shade of boughs.
Happy is he who has found the power to learn   490

The causes of things, and who has trampled down
All terrors, and inexorable doom
Beneath his feet, and hungry Acheron's wailing.
Yet he also is fortunate who knows
The rustic deities, both Pan and that old
Silvanus, and the sisterhood of the Nymphs.
By no honours the people can bestow,
By no purple of kings can he be moved,
Nor yet by civil discord maddening treacherous
Brethren, nor by the Dacian swarming down
From his confederate Danube; not by the State
Of Rome, nor by the death-throes of great kingdoms.
The pangs of pity, beholding poverty,
Never has he known, nor envy of the rich.
What fruits the woodlands or his kindly fields   500
Bear of their own free will, he gathers these;
The iron laws, the Forum's frenzied turmoil,
The public archives, never has he looked on.
Others tempt undiscovered seas with the oar,
Rush on the sword, or press into kings' courts
And antechambers; one will bring destruction
On a whole city and its hapless homes,
That he may drink from a jewelled cup and sleep
On Tyrian purple; another hoards up wealth
And broods o'er buried gold; one with rapt mind
Stares marvelling at the orators; another
Sits open-mouthed, transported by the plaudits
Of people and senators, echoing again
And again along the benches of the theatre.
Gleefully in the spilt blood of their brothers   510
Men bathe their hands; and for a life of exile
Exchanging their dear homes and hearths, they seek
Some land that lies beneath an alien sun.

    Meanwhile the husbandman with his curved plough
Has been furrowing the soil. Thence his year's task;
Thence he wins sustenance for his native land,
For his small grandchildren, his herds of oxen,

And faithful bullocks. Nor is there any pause,
But the year overflows either with fruit,
Or increase of the flocks, or with the sheaves
Of the corn-harvest, loading with its crops
The furrows, and with grain bursting the barns.
Winter is come; in the olive-press the berry
Of Sicyon is crushed; feasted on acorns
The swine come home; arbutes within the woods   520
Are reddening; or it may be autumn is shedding
Its varied fruitage, or among sunny rocks
High up is ripening the mellow vintage.
Meanwhile sweet children crowd round him for kisses;
His chaste home guards its purity; his cows
Droop their milk-laden udders, and fat kids
On the green sward contend horn against horn.
The master himself keeps every holiday,
And stretched out on the grass (while in their midst
The altar flames, and his companions wreathe
The bowl with flowers) he pours libation and calls on thee,
Lord of the winepress; and for the herdsmen marks
An elm for contests of the flying javelin;   530
Or for the rustic wrestling-match they strip
Their hard and sinewy limbs. Such was the life
Lived by the ancient Sabine folk of old,
By Remus and his brother. Thus it was
Etruria grew to strength; and thus did Rome
Come to be fairest of all things that are,
And ringed her seven hills within one wall.
Moreover in the days before the sceptre
Of Cretan Jove, before an impious race
Had learned to banquet upon slaughtered bullocks,
This golden life did Saturn live on earth,
While yet no man had heard the trumpet blare,
Nor the sword ring upon the hard anvil.   540
    But in our course we have traversed with our steeds
A boundless tract of plain, and now 'tis time
To loosen from the yoke their steaming necks.

THE GEORGICS

BOOK THREE

Thee too, great Pales,[1] will I sing, and thee,
Famed shepherd of Amphrysus,[2] and you, streams
And forests of Lycaeus. Other themes,
That once had charmed with song an idle fancy,
To-day are all grown stale. Who has not heard
Of pitiless Eurystheus, and the altars
Of foul Busiris? Who has not told the tale
Of the boy Hylas, of Latona's Delos,
Of Hippodameia, and Pelops renowned
For the ivory shoulder, that keen charioteer?
A path must be essayed by which I too
May have the power to lift myself from earth
And float victorious on the lips of men.
I will be the first, if life but last me,   10
Returning to my native land, to lead
The Muses with me from the Aonian heights.[3]
I will be first to bring thee palms of victory,
My Mantua, and to build a shrine of marble[4]
Upon the green plain by the water's side
Where the broad Mincius winding lazily
Wanders between banks fringed with slender reeds.
Therein shall Caesar stand, my temple's deity.
I in his honour, robed in Tyrian purple,
Will drive triumphantly beside the river
A hundred four-horse chariots. For my games
All Greece, leaving Alpheus and the groves
Of Nemea, shall contend in the foot-race   20

[1] An Italian goddess of flocks and herds.
[2] The pastoral Apollo.   [3] Mount Helicon in Boeotia.
[4] This temple symbolizes the already projected Aeneid.

And with the raw-hide boxing glove; while I,
My brows enwreathed with close-trimmed olive leaves,
Will offer gifts at the altar. What joy now
To watch them lead up to the sanctuary
The solemn pomp, to see the bullocks sacrificed,
To view how the stage opens, while the scenes
Swing round, and how the enwoven Britons raise
The crimson curtain! On the temple doors
I will have carved in gold and solid ivory
That battle with the Orient and the arms
Of conquering Rome; and there too shall be seen
The Nile surging with war, in mighty flood,
And columns rising decked with prows of bronze.
The vanquished towns of Asia will I add,   30
Niphates routed, and the Parthian
Who trusts in flight and arrows backward shot,
And those two trophies wrested in fierce fight
From two far-sundered foes, that double triumph
Over the nations from both coasts of ocean.
Here also breathing images shall stand
In Parian stone, the lineage of Assaracus,[1]
And the great names of that race sprung from Jove,
Father Tros, and the Cynthian God[2] who built
Troy's walls; while hateful Envy shall be seen
Cowering before the Furies and the gloomy
Stream of Cocytus, Ixion's twisted snakes,
His dread wheel, and the unconquerable stone.[3]
Meanwhile let me pursue the virgin glades   40
And forests of the Dryads: no light task
You have laid on me, Maecenas. Uninspired
By you, my spirit essays no lofty theme.
Up then! break through sluggish delays. Cithaeron[4]
With full-voiced cry summons us, and the hounds
From the glens of Taÿgetus, and Argolis

[1] Son of Tros, and mythical ancestor of Julius Caesar.
[2] Apollo.   [3] The stone rolled by Sisyphus.
[4] A mountain in Boeotia.

Tamer of horses—a cry that comes redoubled
By the assenting echoes of the woods.
But erelong will I gird myself to sing
Of Caesar's fiery wars, and bear his name
In story through as many years as Caesar
Is distant from the cradle of Tithonus.[1]
    Whether a man breeds horses, coveting
The prize of the Olympic palm, or breeds
Strong bullocks for the plough, let his chief care   50
Be to choose mothers by their bodily shape.
The best-formed cow is grim-looking, her head
Ugly, her neck thick, with dewlaps that hang
Right down from chin to legs; her long flank too
Will have no end to it; all things large about her,
Even her feet; and under crumpled horns
Are shaggy ears. Well content would I be
If she were marked with white spots, or rebellious
Against the yoke, and sometimes dangerous with her horn;
More like a bull in face, her whole frame tall,
With a tail that sweeps her footprints as she goes.
The age for child-birth and the rites of Hymen   60
Begins after the fourth year, and is over
Before the tenth; from that time they become
Useless for breeding and too weak for the plough.
Meantime, while in your cattle lusty youth
Is still unspent, let loose the males among them;
Be the first to set free your herd for love's
Sweet intercourse, and so renew your stock
By generation following generation.
Life's fairest days for miserable mortals
Are ever the first to flee; on creep diseases
And melancholy old age and suffering,
Till stern death's cruelty hurries us away.
Always there will be some that you would gladly
Replace by younger cows: always renew them;

[1] A Trojan prince, brother of Priam.

And lest too late you should regret your losses,   70
Forestall them, and for the herd choose new stock yearly.
   For breeding horses a like choice is needed:
Only, upon those stallions you propose
To rear in hope of progeny, be sure
To spend your chief pains from their tender youth.
See, from the first how a colt of noble breed
Steps higher in the pasture, and how lightly
He brings his feet down. Boldly he leads the way,
Braves threatening rivers, dares to entrust his weight
To an unknown bridge, starts not at idle noises.
He carries his neck high; his head is shapely;
Short is his belly, and his back full-fleshed;   80
His gallant breast ripples with brawny sinews.
For colour, the best are bay and grey; the worst
Are white and dun. Such a colt, if from afar
He hear the sound of arms, stand still he cannot,
But pricks his ears, quivering in all his limbs,
And snorting breathes his pent fire through his nostrils.
His mane is thick, and when he tosses it,
Falls back on the right shoulder. Along his loins
There runs a double ridge: his hoof scoops out
The ground with a heavy thud of solid horn.
Such was that Cyllarus who learnt to obey
The rein of Pollux of Amyclae; such
Those steeds of Mars, whose fame by Grecian poets   90
Is told; and such the team of great Achilles.
Such too was Saturn, when at his wife's approach
Galloping swiftly he shook out his mane
Over his horse's neck, and filled the heights
Of Pelion with loud neighings as he fled.[1]
   Even such a horse, once he begins to fail
Worn with disease or grown sluggish through years,
Shut up indoors; deal not too leniently
With his inglorious age. For age is cold

[1] Saturn, loving the Nymph Philyra, and being surprised with her by
his wife Ops, fled away in the form of a horse.

To love, and drags on vainly a fruitless task.
In love's encounters, as in a stubble field
Sometimes a great fire rages without strength,
His rage too will be futile. Therefore note   100
Beyond all else their spirit and their youth;
Then other qualities, and the pedigree
Of sire and dam, and the grief each one shows
In defeat, or his pride in victory.
Have you not seen, when bursting from their stalls
The chariots stream forth, swallowing the plains
In headlong rivalry; when now the hopes
Of the young charioteers are at their height,
And throbbing fear drains each exultant heart?
With eager hand they ply the curling lash,
Bending forward to slacken rein: on flies
Fiercely the glowing wheel. Now they sink low;
Now lifted high they seem to ride through empty air
Mounted upon the wind. No stint, no stay.   110
A yellow sand-cloud rises; with the foam
And breath of their pursuers they are wet.
So strong their love of fame, so dear is victory.

    Erechtheus was the first who dared to yoke
Four horses to the car, and stand triumphant
Above the rushing wheels. Thessalian Lapiths,
Mounting the horse's back, gave us the bridle
And ring-riding, and taught the armoured horseman
To spurn the earth, gathering his proud paces.
Each task is arduous alike; for each
Trainers will seek a stallion that is young,
Both hot of spirit and a swift galloper;
Although some older steed may many a time   120
Have driven the foe in flight; although his birthplace
Should be Epirus or renowned Mycenae,
And back to Neptune's self he trace his lineage.

    These points first noted, as the time draws near,
The trainers get to work, and take all heed
To fill out with firm fat the stallion

Whom they have chosen as leader and appointed
Lord of the herd. They cut him flowering herbage,
And bring him water from the stream, and corn,
Lest to his joyous task he prove unequal,
And lest a weakling offspring reproduce
The leanness of their sires. As for the mares,
They starve them purposely to make them thin,
And soon as they perceive the signs that pleasure   130
Is prompting them to union, they withhold
Their leafy fodder and fence them from the streams.
Also they often wear them out with galloping,
And tire them in the sun, while the floor groans
Heavily as the corn is threshed, and while
The empty chaff is tossed to the rising Zephyr.
This they do lest the genital field by pampering
Be dulled for use, or lest the sluggish furrows
Be clogged; but that the soil may thirstily
Seize on the seed and store it deep within.

   But soon care for the sires begins to wane,
And the dams need attention most, when now,
Their months well-nigh fulfilled, they wander pregnant.
Then let none suffer them to draw the yokes   140
Of heavy wains, or leap across the road,
Or race over the meadows at full speed,
Or swim in rushing streams. On open lawns
They pasture them, and beside brimming rivers,
Where there is moss, and on the bank the grass
Is greenest, where are caves to shelter them,
And rock-shadows lie stretched upon the ground.
Among the groves of Silărus and Alburnus
With ilex ever green, there swarms a fly
Whose Roman name is Asĭlus, but the Greeks
In their speech call it Oestrus; a fierce fiend
With harsh loud hum, whereat whole herds are scared
In wild flight through the trees: their bellowings   150
Madden the startled air, and the woods and banks
Of the parched Tanäger. With this monster once

Did Juno wreak her horrible wrath, devising
How to torment Io, the heifer-maiden.
From this too (for more savage is its sting
At burning noon) protect your breeding herd,
Grazing them when the sun is newly risen
Or when the stars are ushering in the night.

　After birth, all care passes to the calves.
At once they brand tokens to mark the stock
On those they have chosen out to rear for breeding,
Or those they would keep sacred for the altar,　　　160
Or else would train to cleave the soil, upturning
The field, till it is rough with broken clods.
While the main herd grazes in green pastures,
Those oxen you would break in for the tasks
And services of husbandry, you must school
While yet calves, entering on the path of training
When their young minds are docile and their age
Is pliant still. And first about their shoulders
Fasten loose rings of slender osier; next,
When their free necks grow used to servitude,
Linking these collars, yoke in pairs your bullocks,
And so compel them to keep step together.
Then let them often draw unloaded wheels　　　170
That print light tracks behind them in the dust.
Last let the beechen axle creak beneath
A huge load, while the brass-bound pole drags on
The coupled wheels. Meanwhile for your unbroken
Young beasts you must not gather grasses only,
Slim willow-leaves and sedges from the marsh,
But hand-plucked standing corn. Nor shall your cows
Who have just calved, fill the pails white with milk
As in our fathers' days, but shall spend all
Their udders on their own dear progeny.

　But if your bent be rather towards battles
And fierce squadrons, or else to glide on wheels
By the streams of Alpheus,[1] and to drive　　　180

[1] Where the Olympian games were held.

6-2

Your swift cars past the grove of Jupiter,
Then the steed's first task is to view the fury
Of armed warriors, and to endure the sound
Of clarions, and the groan of the dragged wheel,
And the jingling of harness in his stall.
Then more and more he takes delight to hear
His master praise him with caressing voice,
And when his neck is patted, loves the sound.
So soon as from his mother's milk he is weaned,
Such trials he must venture; and at times
Must yield his mouth to soft halters, while still
Weak and unsteady, ignorant still of life.
But when three springs are past and the fourth come,   190
At once let him begin to pace the ring
With feet that fall in rhythm, and legs gathered
Into a curve alternately, as though
Disciplined to his task. Now let him challenge
The winds to race with him; now in swift flight
Over open plains, as though free from the bridle,
Let him scarce print his footsteps on the soil:
As when the pregnant north wind, swooping down
From Hyperborean coasts, drives on before him
The storms and rainless clouds of Scythia;
First the deep cornfields and the billowy plains
Shiver beneath light gusts; and soon the tree-tops
Are roaring, and long waves are shoreward surging;   200
On flies the wind scouring both land and sea.
Such a horse will race sweating past the pillars
And down the long laps of the Elēan plain
With bloodily foaming mouth; or else, more gracefully,
With docile neck will draw the Belgic car.
Then only, when the colts are broken in,
Feed them on fattening mash, whereby their bodies
May grow to their full bulk; else before breaking
They will become too proud and mettlesome,
And refuse to endure the supple lash,
When harnessed, or to obey the cruel curb.

But nothing so confirms their strength as carefully
To shield them from the stings of secret love,   210
Whether our preference be for rearing oxen
Or horses. Therefore afar to lonely pastures
We banish bulls, beyond the barrier
Of some hill or broad river, or keep them stalled
Beside full mangers: for as they gaze on her,
The female slowly wastes and burns away
Their strength; nor does she by her sweet allurements
Suffer them to remember woods and pastures;
And often she compels her proud lovers
To decide rivalries by push of horn.
In Sila's mighty forest[1] a lovely heifer
Is grazing. Round her the bulls turn by turn   220
Wage violent battle, dealing many a wound,
Till dark blood bathes their bodies; horn against horn
They charge mightily bellowing, while the woods
And the vast sky re-echo wide and far.
Nor are the champions wont to stall together;
But the defeated bull retires to dwell
Far off, an exile in sequestered wilds,
With many a moan lamenting his disgrace
And the wounds dealt by his proud conqueror,
Lamenting too his love whom unavenged
He is losing: then with a last look at his stall
He has gone, abandoning his ancestral realm.
So all his care is now to train his strength,
And on a couch unstrewn, among hard rocks   230
Nightlong he lies, feeding on prickly leaves
And sharp reed-grass. Soon will he prove himself,
And learn to throw his rage into his horn,
Lunging at tree-trunks, lashing the wind with blows,
Pawing the soil as prelude for the fray.
Last, when his powers are mustered and his strength
Renewed, moving his standard he breaks camp

[1] A forest in Bruttium near the Straits of Messina.

And charges headlong his unmindful foe.
Thus, far away in the mid sea, a wave
Begins to whiten, drawing from the deep
Its curving mass, and rolling to the land
Roars terribly among the rocks; then bursts
Huge as a very mountain, and falls prone;
While from below the water in foaming eddies   240
Boils up and flings aloft the murky sand.

  For every race on earth, whether of men,
Or wild beasts, or the tribes of ocean, cattle,
And gay-plumed birds, into this fiery madness
Rush headlong. For them all, love is the same.
And at no other season does the lioness
Forgetful of her cubs prowl through the wilds
More fiercely; never else do monstrous bears
Spread death and havoc through the woods so widely.
Then is the boar savage, the tigress then
Most fell. Ay me! then folly it were to wander
Through Libya's desert wilderness alone.
See you not how horses are set trembling   250
In all their limbs, if but the winds have brought them
The scent they know so well? No longer now
May a rider's rein and cruel lash have power
To check their course, nor rocks nor beetling crags,
Nay, nor opposing rivers that tear up
And whirl mountainous boulders down their flood.
Behold the rage of the great Sabine boar,
How he whets his tusks and tramples the earth before him,
And rubs his sides against a tree, now this way,
Now that, hardening his shoulders against wounds!
What of the youth, within whose bones the heat
Of ruthless Love has kindled a great flame?
See, late in the black night, he swims the straits
Troubled by bursting storms. Above his head   260
Heaven's mighty portal thunders, and the waves
That dash against the rocks cry out in answer;
Nor can his wretched parents call him back,

Nor the maiden, who by a cruel death must die.
What of the spotted lynxes dear to Bacchus,
The savage tribes of wolves and dogs, the battles
Waged by unwarlike stags? The rage of mares
Surely exceeds all others. Nay, it was Venus
Herself inspired their frenzy, when the limbs
Of Glaucus were devoured by his chariot-steeds.
Love it is leads them over Gargarus,
Across roaring Ascanius: the mountains   270
They scale, they swim the rivers: and when once
Love's flame has stolen into their craving marrow
(In spring most often, for in spring love's heat
Re-enters them), they all, with faces turned
Towards the west wind, stand on rocky heights
And drink in the light breezes; and oft-times
Without coition pregnant with the wind
(A wondrous tale!), over boulders and rocks
They scatter in flight, and down deep-sunken vales,
Not towards the east wind's rising, nor the sun's,
But to the North or the North-west, or where
The South, blackest of winds, is born, to sadden
The face of heaven with his chilly rain.
Then and then only from the groin there trickles   280
That poisonous gum, by shepherds rightly named
'Horse-madness,' which fell stepdames often gather
And mingle with it herbs and baleful charms.
    But time is flying, flying past recall,
While lovingly and lingeringly I dwell
On every detail. Enough now of herds:
Half of my work remains, the management
Of the wool-bearing flock, and shag-haired goats.
Here is labour indeed; here hope for praise,
You sturdy peasants. Nor am I unaware
How hard my task to win this victory
With words, and crown with glory a lowly theme;   290
But rapt by a sweet desire I climb the lonely
Steeps of Parnassus; and thence joyfully

Descend a gentle bypath, that no foot
Has trodden before, to the Castalian spring.
　　Now, revered Pales, now in lofty strain
Must my discourse proceed. First I decree
That in soft-littered pens the sheep be fed
On herbs, till leafy summer soon returns,
And that you strew the hard ground under them
With fern in handfuls and abundant straw,
Lest chilling frost should harm the tender flock
Engendering the mange or foul foot-rot.
Thence passing on, I order that the goats　　　　300
Be given plenteous store of arbute leaves
And supplied with fresh water from the stream:
And let their pens be sheltered from the winds,
Turned towards the south to face the winter sun,
At that time when the Water-carrier sets
Sprinkling with cold showers the departing year.
Goats you must shield with no less care than sheep:
As great will be your profit, how high soever
May be the price paid for Milesian fleeces
In Tyrian purple steeped. From goats there comes
A progeny more numerous; from them
Wealth of abundant milk: the more your pails
Have foamed from the drained udder, the more richly
Will flow the streams when next the teats are pressed.　　310
Meanwhile see to it that they clip the beard
On the white chin of the Cinyphian goat,
And shear his shaggy hair for the use of camps,
Or as covering for miserable seamen.
Among the woods and highlands of Lycaeus
They browse upon the prickly briars and brakes
That love steep slopes; and of themselves they are mindful
To return home leading their kids, and scarce
Can lift their heavy udders o'er the threshold.
Therefore, the less they need the care of men,
With the more zeal from frost and snowy winds
Should you protect them, and with liberal hand　　　　320

Bring them their provender of leafy twigs,
And all through winter keep your hay-lofts open.
But when the zephyrs call, and genial spring
Sends both our sheep and goats to the glades and meadows,
Then at the rising of the morning-star
Haste we to the cool pastures, while the day
Is young, and the grass hoar, and on the tender
Herbage the dew is sweetest to the flocks.
But when the fourth hour has brought thirst to all,
And plaintive crickets thrill the woods with song,
By wells or by deep pools the flock should stand
And drink the water running in troughs of ilex.   330
But in the noonday heat you must seek out
Some shady valley where with ancient trunk
The mighty oak of Jove spreads out his boughs,
Or where some grove, by many an ilex darkened,
Broods with its sacred shadow on the ground.
Then once more let them drink the trickling water,
And once more feed them about set of sun,
When the cool evening star allays the air,
When dews now falling from the moon revive
The pastures, and with the halcyon's cry the shores
Are echoing, with the warbler's song the brakes.
    Why should my verse describe to you those shepherds
Of Libya, their pastures, their encampments   340
Of scattered huts? Often a whole month through
All day and night the flock moves grazing onward
Into an endless wilderness, where no shelters
Are found: so vast and far the plains lie stretched.
All his wealth does the herdsman of Africa
Take with him—house and household gods, his weapons,
His dog, his quiver—like the strenuous legionary,
Equipped in Roman fashion, when beneath
A cruel load he hastes upon his march,
And, ere his foe is ready for him, stands
In line of battle, his camp behind him pitched.
    Far different are the customs of those tribes

Of Scythians dwelling by the Maeotic lake,
Where turbid Danube rolls his yellow sands,   350
And Rhodope bends backward, stretching up
Under the North pole. There they keep their herds
Penned up in stalls, and on the plains no grass
Is seen, nor leaf on tree, but far and wide
The land lies shapeless under mounded snow
And piles of ice, rising seven cubits high.
Always winter, always the cold breath
Of north-west winds. There never does the sun
Scatter the pale mists, not when he mounts his car
To climb the heights of heaven, nor when he laves
His headlong wheels in Ocean's ruddy floor.
Sudden crust forms upon the running river;   360
And soon the water carries on its back
Iron-bound wheels: a welcome once it gave
To ships, now to broad waggons. Everywhere
Brass vessels burst; clothes stiffen on men's backs,
And with an axe they chop the liquid wine;
Whole lakes are frozen solid, and sharp icicles
Harden on unkempt beards. No less meanwhile
All the air is filled with snow; the cattle perish;
Huge oxen stand sheathed round with frost; the deer
Huddle in troops, benumbed by the strange burden
Of snow, above which scarce emerge their antlers.   370
On these they unleash no hounds, nor into nets
Chase them, nor scare with crimson-feathered cord,
But, while their breasts against the piled up snow
Are pushing vainly, stab them with the knife
And slaughter them as they bellow miserably,
Then with loud shouts of triumph bear them home.
Themselves in caves deep-dug within the earth
Living at careless ease roll to the hearth
Logs from the wood-pile, nay whole elms to feed the fire.
So here they pass the long night hours in play,
With ale and bitter juice of service-berries
Jovially counterfeiting draughts of wine.   380

Such is the lawless race of men that dwell
Beneath the seven stars of the utmost North,
By blasts from the Rhipaean mountains buffeted,
Their bodies wrapped in tawny hides of beasts.

    If you breed sheep for wool, let them avoid
Brambles and burrs and caltrops: shun rich pastures;
And always choose white sheep with soft fleeces.
But for the ram, how white so e'er he be,
If only beneath the moist roof of his mouth
His tongue be black, reject him, lest he stain
The coats of your young lambs with dusky spots;
And from your teeming fields choose out some other.   390
It was thus, with a gift of snow-white wool,
If we may trust the tale, that Pan, the god
Of Arcady, charmed and inveigled thee,
O Lady Moon, calling thee to the depths
Of the dark woods; nor didst thou spurn his call.

    But he whose chief wish is for milk, let him
With his own hand carry lucerne and lotus
In plenty, and salted herbage to the stalls.
Thus the more eagerly will they drink from streams,
And the more swell their udders; while a hidden
Flavour of salt will lurk within their milk.
Many bar from their dams the new-born kids,
And at once on their mouths fix iron-bound muzzles.
The milk they draw at dawn or in the hours   400
Of daylight, that they press at night; the milk
They draw at dusk and sundown, that in baskets
They carry away at daybreak (for it is then
The shepherd goes to the town); or else they add
A touch of salt and lay it by for winter.

    Do not neglect the care of dogs, but feed
Both fierce Molossians and swift Spartan whelps
On fattening whey. Never with them to guard you
Need you fear for your pens a midnight thief,
Or the wolf's onslaught, or a stealthy raid
Of lawless brigands. Often will you chase

The shy wild ass, and course the hare with hounds,
With hounds the doe. Oft from his forest wallow   410
The wild boar will you rout, driving him forth
With baying dogs; or over the hills will hunt
A huge stag at full cry into your nets.

   Also burn fragrant cedar in your stalls,
And see to it that with fumes of Syrian gum
You chase away the noisome water-snakes.
Often beneath sheds long uncleansed a viper
Deadly to touch has lurked, shrinking in fear
Of daylight; or an adder, that dire plague
Of oxen, who beneath the roof is wont
To shelter and dart his venom at the cattle,
May be found nestling in the ground. Snatch up,   420
Shepherd, snatch stones and staves, and as he rises
Threatening, and swells his hissing throat, down with him!
And now he has buried deep his frighted head
In flight, while his last coils are still untwining,
And the last fold is trailing its slow curves.
There is too in Calabria's glades that evil snake
Who wreathes his scaly back with neck uplifted,
And his long belly mottled with great spots.
So long as any streams gush from their founts,
So long as earth is wet with the moist spring
And showery southern winds, he haunts the pools,
And dwelling on the banks, there greedily   430
Fills his black maw with fish and chattering frogs.
But when the marsh is baked and the soil gapes
With heat, he darts forth to the land, and rolling
His fiery eyes rages about the fields,
Savage with thirst and by the hot glare frenzied.
Never then may I seek to woo soft sleep
Beneath an open sky, or in the grass
Upon some wooded ridge to lie outstretched,
When fresh from his cast slough, glistening with youth,
Leaving his eggs or hatched brood in his nest,
He glides along, towering towards the sun,

Flickering in his mouth his three-forked tongue.
    Of various diseases must I now   440
Instruct you, of their causes and their signs.
Foul mange attacks the sheep, when the cold rains
And winter rough with hoar frost have soaked through
Deep to the quick, or when the sweat, unwashed,
Has clung to their shorn skins, and prickly briars
Have torn their flesh. Therefore the shepherds bathe
The whole flock in fresh streams: the ram, plunged in,
Goes floating down the current with drenched fleece.
Or else with bitter oil-lees after shearing
They anoint their bodies, and blend silver-scum
With natural sulphur, or with pitch from Ida,   450
Or wax softened with oil, or sea-onions,
With potent hellebore and black bitumen.
Yet for their troubles there can be no cure
So helpful as when some shepherd dares to cut
The head of the ulcer open with his knife.
The mischief lives and thrives upon concealment,
Whilst he refuses to lay healing hands
Upon the wound, and sits praying the gods
For happier omens. Nay when the pain has pierced
To the very marrow of the bleating sheep,
And parching fever is preying on their limbs,
It may prove wise to allay the burning heat
By lancing a vein throbbing with blood between   460
The hoofs; as is the wont of the Bisaltae,
And of the fierce Gelonian, when their tribes
Migrate to Rhodope, or the Getan solitudes,
And there drink milk curdled with horse's blood.
If you should see a sheep that oft withdraws
Aloof into luxurious shade, or listlessly
Browses the grass-tips, lagging behind the flock,
Or as it grazes sinks down in mid-field,
And comes home late at nightfall and alone,
Check with your knife the danger, and at once,
Ere the dread taint spread through the heedless throng.

A storm-wind o'er the sea sweeps not so swiftly   470
As in the flock diseases multiply.
Not single victims do plagues snatch away,
But a whole summer's folding at one stroke,
The flock together with the flock's young hope,
The whole race, root and branch. Hereof let those
Be witness, who may visit—even now,
After so long a time—the soaring Alps,
The Noric hill-forts and Timavus' stream,
And look upon the shepherds' realms unpeopled,
And their glades far and wide untenanted.
　　Here once from the distempered air there came
A disastrous season, glowing with all the heat
Of autumn, and delivered up to death
Whole generations of beasts, tame and wild,   480
Contaminating pools, infecting pastures
With pestilence. Nor was the road to death
Uniform; but when fiery thirst, coursing
Through every vein, had shrunk the afflicted limbs,
A change came: watery fluid overflowed,
Into itself absorbing all the bones
Piecemeal, as by disease they were dissolved.
Often during the worship of the gods
The victim, while it stood beside the altar,
And while the fillet with its snow-white garland
Was being twined around its head, fell dying
Amid the tardy ministrants. Or if
The priest's knife had already slain a victim,
No flame rose from the entrails laid on the altars,   490
Nor could the seer respond to questioners;
The blood scarce stains the knife beneath the throat,
And only the surface of the sand is darkened
By the thin gore. And now on every side
Amid luxuriant grass the calves are dying,
Or by full mangers yielding up sweet life.
Now upon gentle dogs fierce madness falls;
The swine sicken, racked by a gasping cough

Which chokes the breath within their swollen throats.
The steed, once victor, his skill and prowess gone,
Stands tottering, and forgetful of the grass
Turns from the stream, and often paws the ground;
His ears droop; and upon them fitfully   500
A sweat breaks out, cold as his death draws near;
His skin feels dry and hard to the stroking hand.
Such at first are the signs that prelude death.
But when as it advances the disease
Grows fiercer, then their eyes are ablaze, deep-drawn
Their breath, laden from time to time with moans;
Their flanks and bellies with a long deep sob
Heave; from their nostrils gushes forth black blood,
And the rough tongue chokes the obstructed throat.
Sometimes it was thought helpful to thrust in
A horn and through it pour a draught of wine.
Such seemed the only hope to save the dying.   510
Soon even this remedy brought death; they burned
With revived fury, and though now in the weakness
Of death (may Heaven reserve a happier fortune
For good men, and such madness for their foes!),
With bared teeth rent and mangled their own limbs.
   But lo, the bull, sweating beneath the heavy plough,
Falls, spurting from his mouth blood mixed with foam,
Uttering his last moanings. Sick at heart
The ploughman goes to unyoke the steer who stands
Sorrowing for his brother's death; then leaves
The share fixed in the soil, its task unfinished.
No longer may the shade of the deep wood   520
Nor the soft meadows bring joy to his heart
Nor yet the stream that rushing through the rocks
More pure than amber hastens to the plain;
But his flanks are all unstrung; a dimness falls
Upon his languid eyes, and slowly drooping
His neck sinks heavily down onto the earth.
What avail toil and service? What avails it
To have turned the stiff soil with the share? And yet

No choice wine from the vineyards of Campania,
No banquets oft renewed, did harm to him
And to his kind. For them a feast it is
To feed on leaves and simple grass; their cups
Are clear springs and streams racing as they run;
And by no cares their healthful sleep is broken.   530
   Never before, they say, in those regions
Were oxen sought in vain for Juno's rites,
Nor were cars drawn by ill-matched buffaloes
To her lofty temples. Therefore painfully
Men scrape the earth with hoes, burying the seed
With their own nails, and over the high hills
With straining necks must drag their creaking wains.
No longer stealthily round the sheepfold slinks
The wolf, nor by night prowls about the flocks:
A crueller care has tamed him. The shy deer
And timorous stags now stray among the dogs   540
And round houses. The brood of the vast deep
And all the tribes of swimming creatures lie,
Like shipwrecked corpses, washed up by the waves
On the shore's margin: seals in rivers find
Unwonted refuge. And the viper too,
Vainly defended by her winding lairs,
Perishes, and the water-snake, his scales
Erect in terror. To the very birds
The air becomes unkindly, and they drop
Leaving their life beneath the clouds on high.
Furthermore change of food avails no more:
The remedies invoked work harm: defeated
Are those great masters, Cheiron and Melampus.[1]   550
Sent forth into the light from Stygian glooms
Rages ghastly Tisiphone, and drives
Panic and Plague before her, and day by day
Towering lifts more high her ravenous head.
Ever with flocks bleating and cattle lowing
Rivers and parched banks and low hills resound.

[1] Mythical physicians.

And now in droves the Fury deals destruction
And heaps the very pens with carcases
Rotting with putrid foulness, till men learn
To cover them with earth and hide them in pits.
For neither can the skins be used, nor may
The flesh be cleansed by water or cooked by fire.   560
They cannot shear the fleeces, eaten up
With sores and filth, nor touch the rotting web:
Nay, if a man dared don the loathsome garment,
Feverish pustules and foul sweat would run
Over his evil-smelling limbs; nor long
Had he to wait before the 'accursed fire'[1]
Was feeding on his contaminated body.

[1] Erysipelas.

THE GEORGICS

BOOK FOUR

My next task is to tell of Heaven's gift,
The honey from the skies.[1] Here, as before,
Maecenas, look with favour on my travail.
Now must you marvel at the spectacle
Of a tiny commonwealth; great-hearted chiefs,
The manners and pursuits of a whole nation,
Its tribes and battles, in order will I show you.
The toil is on a slight theme; but not slight
The glory, if adverse deities allow,
And to my prayer Apollo deign to listen.
    First must a site be chosen for your bees,
Whither the winds may not encroach (for winds
Suffer them not to carry home their food),
And where no ewes and butting kids may trample   10
The flowers, nor heifer straying through the field
Brush off the dew and crush the springing grass.
And let no scaly lizard's mottled back
Be seen near their rich homesteads, nor bee-eaters
And other such birds, nor the swallow, Procne,
Her breast marked by her blood-stained hands; for they
Spread havoc far and wide, and while the bees
Are on the wing, snatch them off in their mouths
A delicate morsel for their cruel nestlings.
But let clear springs be near, and moss-green pools,
And stealing through the grass a shallow rill;
And let a palm or huge wild-olive shade   20

---

[1] It was believed that honey fell from heaven as a dew. Under Saturn's
reign this honey-dew was very plentiful; but, when the golden age
ended, Jupiter 'shook the honey from the leaves' (Georgics, 1, 131),
whence the bees now laboriously collect what little they can find of it.

The porch; that so, when the new kings lead forth
The first swarms in their own Spring, and the youth
Issuing from the comb sport to and fro,
The stream's bank may be there inviting them
To a refuge from the sun's heat, and the tree
With hospitable leaves may give them shelter.
Into the water's midst, whether it be
Stagnant or flowing, fling athwart it willows
And big stones, that there may be many bridges
For them to rest upon and spread their wings
To the summer sun, if perchance an east wind
Have sprinkled them, while loitering, with a shower,
Or with swift gust have plunged them in the mere.
All around let green cassia grow, and thyme   30
With its far-spreading fragrance, and a wealth
Of heavy-scented savory, and let beds
Of violets drink from the plashing rill.
The hives themselves moreover, whether stitched
Of hollow cork, or woven of pliant osier,
Should have narrow entrances; for with its cold
Winter congeals the honey; while heat melts
And makes it run. Both dangers for your bees
Are alike to be feared: nor without cause
Industriously do they smear with wax
Each tiny crevice in their hive, and fill
The chinks with paste from flowers, and keep a store
Of glue they have gathered for this purpose, stickier   40
Than bird-lime, or than pitch from Phrygian Ida.
Often too, if the tales we have heard be truth,
In hiding-places tunnelled under the earth
They make themselves warm homes, and have been found
Deep in the hollows of a porous rock,
Or in the cave of a decaying tree.
Yet must you give their crannied chambers warmth
Smearing them with smooth clay, and over them
Spread a thin coat of leaves. Do not allow
A yew tree near the hive; nor should you burn

Scarlet crabs on the hearth; and put no trust
In a deep marsh, or where the smell of mud
Is strong, or where curved rocks reverberate
A sound that strikes them, and fling back the echo.   50
   Now when the golden sun has driven the winter
Beneath the earth defeated, and revealed
The sky with summer light, straightway they rove
Through glades and woods, pillaging the gay flowers,
And sip the stream's surface on hovering wing.
Therefore, glad with some sweet mysterious joy,
Their nestling young they cherish; artfully
They forge fresh wax and mould the clammy honey.
And so, when looking up you see their host,
Escaped from prison towards the starry sky,
Swim through the liquid summer air, and marvel
At the dark cloud floating upon the wind,   60
Watch them well: brooks and pools of sweet water
And leafy shades ever will they be seeking.
Here you must sprinkle the odours I prescribe,
Crushed balm and lowly tufts of honeywort;
Then you must raise a tinkling sound and clash
The Mighty Mother's cymbals round about.
Of themselves on the scented resting place
Soon will they settle; of themselves will hide
After their wont within their secret cradles.
   But if for battle they have issued forth—
For often strife with mighty tumult rises
Between two kings, and at once from afar
You may divine the fury of the crowd,
And how their hearts are trembling for the fray;   70
For now that martial note as of harsh brass
May be heard chiding loiterers, and a sound
Like broken trumpet-blasts—then eagerly
They flock together; their wings flash; they whet
Their stings upon their beaks, and brace their sinews,
And round their king, thronging his royal tent,
They swarm, with loud cries challenging the foe.

And now, when they have found a clear spring day
And open battle-field, forth from the gates
They burst; they rush together; high in air
Is heard a noise; they are mingled and conglobed
Into one great ball; then they tumble headlong.
No thicker from the skies does hail come pelting, 80
Or acorns raining from the shaken oak.
The chiefs on splendent wings move through the ranks,
With giant souls inspiring pigmy breasts,
Still steadfast not to yield, till the overpowering
Conqueror has compelled this host or that
To turn their backs in flight. These stormy passions,
These mighty conflicts, if a little dust
Be tossed upon them, are quelled and laid to rest.
    When from the fray you have recalled both captains,
The one who appears inferior, lest his wastefulness
Bring ruin, him deliver to the death:
Without a rival let the nobler reign. 90
The one will glow with markings of gold mail:
For there are two kinds; this the better far,
Splendid of mien and bright with ruddy scales;
Squalid from sloth the other, ignobly dragging
A broad paunch. As in aspect the two kings
Differ, so do the bodies of their peoples.
For the one sort are ugly and unkempt,
As when out of deep dust a wayfarer
Comes parched, and spits the dirt from his dry mouth.
The others glint and flash resplendently,
Ablaze with gold and flecked with equal spots.
This is the worthier breed; and from their combs 100
In heaven's due season you will press sweet honey;
Yet not sweet only, but both clear and fit
To subdue the harsh flavour of your wine.
    But when your swarms are flying aimlessly
Disporting in the sky, scorning their cells
And leaving their hives cold, you must restrain
Their fickle spirit from such idle play.

Nor is restraint a hard task. Do but tear
From the chieftains their wings: while they at home
Are hiding, none will dare to soar aloft,
Or to pluck up the standards from the camp.
A garden let there be to invite them, fragrant
With saffron flowers; and let guardian Priapus,
Lord of the Hellespont, watchman against thieves   110
And birds, protect them with his willow sickle.
Himself let the beekeeper bring pine saplings
And thyme from the high hills, and plant them widely
Around the hives; himself with stern labour
Harden his hands, himself within the soil
Set fruitful slips, and sprinkle kindly showers.
    And in truth, but that now I am drawing near
The extreme goal of my task, furling my sails,
And hastening to turn my prow to land,
Haply I had told you of the care wherewith
Rich garden soil must be tilled and adorned,
And of the rosaries of twice-bearing Paestum;
How the endive rejoices in the stream   120
It drinks from, and the green bank in the parsley;
How winding through the grass the cucumber
Swells to a paunch; nor had I passed in silence
Late-flowering narcissus, or the curled
Acanthus, pallid ivy, or the myrtle
That loves the sea-shore. For I well remember
How once, under the high towers of Tarentum,
Where dark Galaesus moistens yellow cornfields,
I saw an old Corycian, who possessed
Some few acres of unclaimed land, a soil
Unfertile for the plough, for pasturage
Ill-suited, and unkindly to the vine.
Yet he, when among the bushes here and there   130
He had planted pot-herbs, and white lilies round them,
Vervain and slender poppy, would match in spirit
The wealth of kings, and coming home at night
Would load his table with an unbought feast.

He was the first in spring to pluck the rose,
Apples in autumn; and while gloomy winter
Was even yet splitting rocks with frost, and curbing
The running streams, there would he be already
Gathering flowers of delicate hyacinth,
Chiding the late spring and the tardy zephyrs.
Therefore he was the first to be enriched
With mother-bees and a big swarm; the first
From the squeezed comb to gather frothing honey.   140
Lime trees he had, and wild laurel in plenty;
And all the fruits wherewith each fertile tree
Had clothed itself in early flowering time,
So many in ripening autumn it still bore.
Moreover he had planted out in rows
Elm trees full-grown, and hard-wood pears, and thorns
Already bearing plums, and planes already
Ministering shade to thirsty wayfarers.
But I, by scanty space debarred, pass by such themes,
And leave for others after me to tell.

Now listen; I will unfold to you the natures
That Jove bestowed on bees; for which reward,   150
Following the tuneful cries and clashing brass
Of the Curetes, in that Cretan cave,
They fed the King of Heaven.[1] They alone
Possess children in common, and share as partners
The dwellings of their city, and lead a life
Under the law's majesty; they alone
Know stablished household gods and fatherland;
And mindful of winter's coming, toil through summer,
Garnering their gains into one common store.
For some are diligent to gather food
And by fixed covenants labour in the field;
Some, as the first foundation of the comb,
Within the house-walls spread tears of narcissus

---

[1] Saturn had the habit of devouring his children, lest they should supplant him. But the infant Zeus was hidden by his mother in a mountain cavern in Crete, where the Curetes drowned his cries by clashing their weapons, while the bees fed him with honey.

And sticky resin from the bark of trees,   160
Then hang therefrom the clinging wax; others
Lead out the full-grown young, the nation's hope;
Others pack purest honey and brim the cells
With liquid nectar. To some it falls by lot
To keep guard at the gates: in turn they watch
For showers and cloudy skies, or take their loads
From incomers, or rank themselves to drive
The drones, that lazy herd, far from the hive.
The work is aglow, and the thyme-scented honey
Breathes fragrance. And as, when the Cyclopes forge   170
Thunderbolts with quick strokes from ductile ore;
Into ox-hide bellows some drink in the air
And blow it forth, others dip hissing bronze
Into the trough, while Aetna groans beneath
The weight of the anvils; they with mighty force,
One now and now another, lift their arms
In rhythm, and turn the iron with gripping tongs:
So, if small things may be compared with great,
An inborn love of having is ever urging
Cecropian bees,[1] each after its own function.
The aged have charge of the towns: 'tis they
Who build the comb, fashioning the curious chambers.
But the young, late at night, wearied with labour   180
Come home, their thighs laden with thyme-pollen:
On arbutus they pasture far and wide,
On pale green willows, cassia, and golden crocus,
Or rich lime-blossom and dusky hyacinths.
For all there is one rest from toil; for all
One work-time. Through the gates at dawn they stream;
Nowhere a loiterer. Again, when once
The star of evening warns them to withdraw
At length from pasturing the meadows, then
They seek their homes, then they refresh their bodies;
A humming sound is heard about the entries

[1] The honey from Hymettus, a thymy hill in Attica (Cecropia) was, and still is, famous.

And on the thresholds. Afterwards when now
They have sunk to rest within their chambers, silence
Deepens with night, and welcome slumber invades   190
Their wearied limbs. Nor yet, when rain is threatening,
Far away from their homesteads do they roam,
Or trust the sky when eastern gales are rising,
But close around their city walls in safety
Fetch water and adventure on short flights,
And, as unsteady boats on tossing waves
Take ballast, often will they lift small stones[1]
Wherewith they poise themselves through void cloudland.

   Moreover you will marvel that with bees
This custom has found favour: they indulge not
In marriage, nor relax their bodies idly
In love's embrace, nor bring forth young with travail,
But alone from the leaves and scented herbage   200
Gather their children in their mouths; alone
Provide a king and tiny citizens,
And mould anew their courts and waxen palaces.
Often too, wandering among rugged rocks,
They bruise their wings, and freely yield their lives
Under the load; so great their love of flowers,
So proud their glory in begetting honey.
Therefore although a narrow span of life
Awaits the bees themselves (for it stretches never
Beyond seven summers), yet the race abides
Immortal, and the fortune of the house
Stands firm through many years, while to the third
And fourth generation sires on sires are numbered.

   Moreover neither Egypt nor great Lydia,   210
Nor Parthia's tribes, nor Median Hydaspes
Pay to their king such reverence. Their king safe,
All are of one mind; when he perishes,
Forthwith they break their fealty, and themselves
Plunder their store of honey, and destroy

---

[1] 'Perhaps a load of pollen was mistaken for gravel.' Sidgwick.

Their trellised combs. He is guardian of their labours;
It is him they revere; their multitudes
Throng close around him in a murmurous swarm;
And often on their shoulders do they lift him,
Or shield him with their bodies from the fray,
And rush through wounds to seek a glorious death.
    Led by these tokens and these instances
Some have asserted that bees have received
A portion of divine intelligence,   220
And draughts of ether: for a deity
There is pervading the whole earth and all
The expanses of the sea, and heights of heaven:
That from him flocks and herds, men and wild beasts
Of every kind, each at its birth drinks in
The subtle breath of life; and thus all beings
Soon return thither, there to be dissolved
And so restored; nor for death is there place;
But, living still, into the ranks of stars
They fly aloft, and find their rest in heaven.
    Whene'er you would unseal their narrow dwelling
And the honey hoarded in their treasuries,
First with a draught of water rinse your mouth,
And blow before you penetrating smoke.   230
Twice do bee-keepers gather the heavy yield;
Twice a year comes their harvest-time: first when
Taÿgete the Pleiad has displayed
Her comely face to the earth, with scornful foot
Spurning the Ocean streams; and when again
Fleeing the rainy Fish's sign, she sinks
Sadly from heaven into the wintry waves.
Their rage is past all measure: if you molest them,
Into their punctures they inject their poison,
And fastening on a vein, there leave their stings
Unseen, and in the wound lay down their lives.
But if you fear the winter's cruelty
And would protect their future, pitying
Their broken spirits and their shattered fortunes,   240

Then who would hesitate to smoke them out
With thyme, and cut away the empty cells?
For oft the newt has nibbled at the combs
Unnoticed, and light-loathing beetles cram
The sleeping-chambers, and the unhelpful drone
Seats himself to devour another's meal;
Or the ferocious hornet has joined battle
Against their ill-matched arms; or moths appear,
A dread race; or Minerva's foe, the spider,
Across the doorway hangs her loose-webbed nets.
The more their storehouses are drained, the more
Eagerly will they labour to repair
The ruins of their fallen commonwealth,
Filling their galleries of cells with honey,
And plundering flowers for wax to build their barns.   250
    But if (since to bees also life must bring
The same mischances as to men) their bodies
Should languish blighted by disease—and this
You may discern by no uncertain signs:
Their colour, as they sicken, at once changes;
A ragged leanness mars their looks; and soon
They are carrying lifeless corpses from their homes,
Escorting gloomy funerals to the grave;
Or else clinging in clusters by their feet
From the doorways they hang; or the whole swarm
Lingers within its dwelling close confined,
Torpid with hunger, numbed with cramping cold.
Then is heard a hoarse noise; in a long-drawn hum   260
They murmur; as at times the cold south wind
Sighs in the forest; as the fretful sea
Growls when the surge flows back; and as within
Closed furnaces the raging fire roars.
Here would I counsel to burn fragrant gums,
And convey to them honey in pipes of reed,
Offering them encouragement and inviting
The languid bees to their familiar food.
Also it will be well to mix therein

The pounded oak-gall's flavour, and dried rose-leaves,
Or new wine boiled thick over a strong fire,
Or juice from clusters of the Psithian vine,
With Attic thyme and pungent centaury.   270
There is a flower[1] too, growing in the meadows—
Amellus is the name the peasants give it—
A plant easy to find, for the stalks rise
In dense tufts from a single clump: bright gold
The centre; but in the petals crowding round it
Beneath dark violet lurks a purple gleam.
Often are the altars of the gods adorned
With its twined garlands: bitter to the mouth
Its savour: shepherds gather it in the valleys
Cropped by their flocks near Mella's winding stream.
Boil its roots in sweet-scented wine, and set them
For food beside their doors in basketfuls.   280
    But for one whose whole breed has failed him suddenly,
So that he knows not how to restore the race
By a new generation, it is time
For me to expound the memorable device
Of the Arcadian master,[2] and the mode
Whereby oft in the past the putrid blood
Of slaughtered bullocks has engendered bees.
The whole tale, tracing it backward to its source,
Will I now tell. For where the fortunate folk
Of Macedonian Canopus dwell
By the outspread waters of the flooded Nile,
And sail about their fields in painted skiffs,
Where quivered Persia's[3] frontier presses close,   290
And where the river, that has flowed straight down
From the dark-coloured Indians,[4] parts its stream

---

[1] The *Aster Atticus* or purple Italian starwort.
[2] Aristaeus, son of Apollo and the Nymph Cyrene, a shepherd and bee-keeper.
[3] The Persian, or Parthian, empires had once been, and would again be, the hostile neighbours of Egypt.
[4] Virgil writes 'Indians', but means 'Ethiopians'.

Into those seven mouths, and makes green Egypt
Rich with black silt—there all bee-keepers build
On this device their sure prosperity.
    First they choose out a site, that must be small
And confined for the purpose. This they roof
With narrow tiling and shut in with walls,
And add four windows through which slanting light
From the four quarters of the sky may enter.
They look then for a bull-calf, with horns curving
Over a forehead of two summers' growth;
Both nostrils and the breath within his mouth   300
Spite of his violent struggling are stopped up;
And when they have beaten him to death, his flesh
To a pulp is pounded through the unbroken hide.
Thus prisoned they leave him, and beneath his ribs
Lay broken branches, thyme and fresh-plucked cassia.
This should be done when Zephyrs are beginning
To impel the waves, before the meadows blush
With spring's new colours, ere yet from the rafters
The chattering swallow hangs her nest. Meanwhile
The moisture, warming in the softened bones,
Ferments, and living creatures marvellous
To look on, without feet at first, but soon   310
With buzzing wings as well, together are swarming,
And more and more essaying the thin air;
Till like a shower pouring from summer clouds
They burst forth, or like flights of arrows, sped
From the rebounding bowstring, when the light
Parthian horse are preluding the battle.
    What God, ye Muses, forged for us this craft?
How arose this new experience for men?
The shepherd Aristaeus, abandoning
Penēan Tempe, when, so runs the tale,
His bees were lost through famine and disease,
Stood sorrowfully beside the sacred source
At the stream's head, and there in long-drawn plaint
Thus did he call on her who gave him birth: 320

'Mother, Cyrene mother, who dost dwell
Within this river's depths, why from the glorious
Race of the Gods (if verily as thou sayest
Thymbraean Apollo is my sire) didst thou
Engender me to be hated by the Fates?
Or whither has thy love for me thy son
Vanished? Why didst thou bid me hope for Heaven?
Lo, even this poor glory of mortal life
(Which hardly and by infinite endeavour
My skilful husbandry of crops and cattle
Had won for me), for all thou art my mother,
I here resign. Nay come, with thine own hand
Uproot my fruitful orchards; into my fold
Cast baneful fire; destroy my corn; burn up   330
My seedlings; against my vines wield the strong axe—
Since you have grown so weary of my honour.'
    But from her chamber beneath the deep river
His mother heard the cry. Round her the Nymphs
Were spinning fleeces dyed with rich sea-green,
Drymo and Xantho, Ligēa and Phyllodocē,
Their bright locks flowing over snowy necks,
And Cydippe and yellow-haired Lycórias
(A maiden was the one; of late the other
For the first time had known Lucina's pangs),   340
And Clio and her sister Beroe,
Daughters of Ocean both, both decked with gold,
Girt both with dappled skins; Ephyrē and Opis,
Asian Deïopēa, and Arethusa,
That fleet huntress, her shafts now laid aside.
And in their midst sat Clymene, recounting
The tale of Vulcan's baffled jealousy,
And of the wiles and stolen joys of Mars;
Narrating too, from chaos downward, all
The innumerable gallantries of the Gods.
But while, enchanted by her song, they twirled
The soft wool with their spindles, yet again
Did the lament of Aristaeus pierce

To his mother's ears, and on their glassy seats   350
All listened wondering. Then of her sister Nymphs
The first was Arethusa to look forth,
Lifting her golden head above the water;
And from afar she cried, 'Cyrene, sister,
Not for naught art thou startled by a moan
So grievous. It is he, thy chiefest care,
Unhappy Aristaeus, who stands weeping
Beside the river of thy sire Penēus,
And calls thee cruel, crying on thy name.'
    To her the mother, heart-struck with strange dread,
'Go, bring him, bring him to us. Lawful it is
For him to tread the threshold of the Gods.'
So saying, she bids the deep streams part asunder
Leaving a broad path for the youth to enter.   360
And lo, curved like a mountain, round him stood
The waters, and within their vast bosom
Received and sped him on beneath the river.
And now, marvelling at his mother's palace
And watery realms, marvelling at cave-roofed pools
And sound-filled groves, he went his way; and dazed
By the huge swirl of waters, stared around
On all the streams of divers lands, there gliding
Under the mighty earth—Phasis and Lycus,
The source whence deep Enipeus first breaks forth,
Whence Father Tiber, whence the brooks of Anio,
And rocky roaring Hypanis, and Caïcus,   370
And bull-faced with his gilded horn, Eridanus,[1]
Than whom no river flows more violently
Through fertile tilth into the dark blue sea.
When he has reached the chamber's hanging roof
Of stone, and Cyrene has learnt the cause
Of her son's idle tears, her sisters duly
Pour clear spring water on his hands, and bring
Towels with close-shorn nap; while others pile

[1] The Po.

The banquet on the table, and in turn
Set on the brimmed cups. With Panchaean spice[1]
The altars blaze. Then says the mother, 'Take   380
Bowls of Maeonian wine: to Oceanus
Pour we libations'. Thereupon she offers
A prayer to Ocean, father of all being,
And to the sisterhood of Nymphs who guard
A hundred forests and a hundred streams.
Thrice with clear nectar the glowing hearth she sprinkles,
Thrice to the roof leapt the bright-glancing flame.
Cheering his heart with the omen, she spoke thus.
   'In the Carpathian deep[2] there dwells a seer,
Sea-green Proteus, who in his chariot, yoked
With steeds two-footed and fish-tailed, is borne
Over the vast sea's plain. He now once more
Is visiting the harbours of Emathia   390
And his birth-place Pallenē. To him we Nymphs
Do reverence, and ancient Nereus too;
For all things the seer knows, all things which are,
And have been, and are drawing near their birth;
So Neptune has ordained, whose monstrous herd
Of foul seals Proteus pastures neath the wave.
Him, son, you must first take and fetter fast,
That so he may unfold to you the whole tale
Of this disease, and grant a prosperous issue.
For without force no counsel will he give,
Nor by prayers will you bend him. With stern force
Bind him fast, and with shackles: on these only
His stratagems will break themselves in vain.   400
I myself, when at length the sun has kindled
His noon-day heat, when the grass is athirst,
And the shade has grown welcome to the flock,
Will guide you to the ancient one's retreat,
Whither, when wearied, from the waves he retires;
Thus easily may you approach him while he lies

---

[1] Arabian incense.   [2] Between Rhodes and Crete.

Sleeping. But when you have caught him in the grip
Of hands and fetters, then will you be mocked
By divers shapes and features of wild beasts.
For suddenly will he change to a bristly boar,
To a grim tiger or a scaly serpent,
Then to a lioness with tawny neck;
Or will give forth the sharp crackling of flame
And so slip from your fetters, or dissolve
Into unsubstantial water and be gone. 410
But the more he changes into every form,
The more, my son, tighten the strangling bonds,
Till, with the last mutation of his body,
He appears once more such as you saw him first
When on his drooping eyelids slumber fell.'
  So saying she pours forth fragrant ambergris
Wherewith her son's whole body she anoints,
While from his smoothed locks a sweet odour breathes,
And into his limbs passes a supple strength.
There is a vast cave eaten out within
A mountain's flank, into which many a wave
Is driven by the wind, there to divide 420
Into receding bays; a roadstead safe
For mariners caught by storms. Within it Proteus
Shelters himself behind a mighty rock.
Here then the Nymph places her son in hiding
Where the light may not reach him: she herself
Withdraws and stands aloof veiled in a mist.
And now the Dog-star, scorching with fierce heat
The thirsty Indians, was ablaze in heaven,
And half his circuit had the fiery Sun
Consumed; the grass was withering; the hot rays
Were scalding the hollow rivers, baking them
In their parched channels down to the very mud;
When Proteus issued from the waves and sought
His wonted cavern: round him the wet tribes 430
Of the great sea gambolling splash about
The salt spray. Then the seals lay themselves down

To slumber here and there along the beach;
Their master—like the guardian of a fold
When the evening star is bringing the calves home
From pasture, and the bleating of the lambs
Is whetting the wolf's hunger—takes his seat
Among them on a rock and tells their tale.
But soon as Aristaeus spies his chance
Of seizing the old man, scarce will he suffer him
To settle down his wearied limbs to rest,
But bursts upon him with a mighty shout,
Surprising him with bonds as there he lies.
But Proteus, not unmindful of his art,   440
Transforms himself into all kinds of marvels,
Into a fire, into a horrible beast,
A flowing river. But when no disguise
Wins him escape, vanquished, to his own form
Returned, he speaks at last through human lips.
'Why, who, most impudent of youths, has bidden you
Invade my home? And what want you from me?'
Then said the youth, 'Proteus, you know; already
You know it; nor in aught may I deceive you.
But cease yourself from wishing to deceive.
Following divine command I come to seek
From you an oracle for my prostrate fortunes.'
Thus he spoke; and the seer, yielding at last   450
To strong compulsion, rolled on him eyes ablaze
With green light, and with fierce gnashing of teeth
Opened his lips, thus to declare Fate's will.
    'Think not there is no God whose wrath pursues you.
Great is the crime for which you pay: this penalty,
Far less than you deserve, miserable Orpheus
Invokes against you—did not Fate oppose—
Still fiercely raging for his ravished bride.
She, hastening headlong by the river's side
To escape your pursuit, before her feet
Saw not in the deep grass, poor death-doomed maiden,
A monstrous serpent lurking on the bank.

But the choir of her Dryad playmates filled   460
The mountain tops with their lament; the crags
Of Rhodope and high Pangaeus[1] wept,
The warrior land of Rhesus, and the Getae,
And the Hebrus, and Actian Orithyia.
But he, solacing on his hollow shell
Love's anguish, of thee would he sing, sweet wife,
Of thee to himself upon the lonely shore,
Of thee at dawn, as daylight failed of thee.
Even the jaws of Taenarus, the lofty
Gateway of Dis,[2] he entered, and the grove
Gloomed with black horror, and approached the Powers
Of Hades and their awful King, those hearts
That know not how to soften at human prayer.   470
Moved by his song forth from the deepest dens
Of Erebus came the unsubstantial shades,
And the phantoms of those bereft of life,
Thousandfold as the birds that hide among
The leaves when the evening star or wintry rain
Sends them home from the hills; matrons and men,
The lifeless ghosts of noble-hearted heroes,
Boys and unwedded maidens, and young men
Laid on the pyre before their parents' eyes;
Whom, all around, the black mud and the loathly
Reeds of Cocytus, and the sluggish waters
Of that unlovely swamp bind fast, and Styx
Imprisons them within his ninefold coils.   480
Nay, spell-bound were the very halls of death,
And the abysm of Tartarus, and the Furies,
Their locks with livid snakes entwined; while Cerberus
Held his three mouths silent, agape; the wind
Ceased, and Ixion's circling wheel stood still.
And now, his steps retracing, every peril
Had he escaped, and his restored Eurydice
Was coming forth into the airs of heaven,

[1] Mountains in Thrace, the land of Rhesus, through which flows the Hebrus.   [2] Pluto.

Following behind (for such the law imposed
By Proserpine), when on her thoughtless lover
Fell sudden madness—worthy of pardon surely,
If but the Powers of Hell knew how to pardon:
He stopped, and on his own Eurydice   490
Within the very threshold of daylight,
Forgetful, alas, and foiled in his resolve,
Looked back. Then spilt was all his toil, and broken
His treaty with that ruthless king; and thrice
Was thunder heard above the Avernian pool.
'What,' cried she, 'what dire madness has destroyed
Both me (ah misery!) and thyself no less,
Orpheus? Lo, once more the relentless Fates
Are summoning me back and sleep is veiling
My dimmed eyes. Now farewell. Wrapt in vast darkness
I am borne away, towards thee stretching forth
These helpless hands, thine own, alas, no longer....'
So said she; and straightway from his sight, like smoke
Mingling with thin air, vanished far away;   500
And, though in vain he clutched at shadows, yearning
For more words, never did she see him more;
Nor did the ferryman of Orcus suffer him
Again to pass the marsh that sundered them.
What should he do? Whither now turn, once more
Reft of his wife? With what tears move Hell's Powers,
Or with what song its Gods?—while she, already
Death-cold, was floating on the Stygian bark.
For seven whole months, one after one, 'tis said,
Beneath a soaring rock beside the waters
Of lonely Strymon under the freezing stars
Weeping he sat and poured forth his despair,
Soothing tigers and moving oaks with song.   510
Thus, mourning in a poplar's shade, the nightingale
Wails for her lost brood, which the ploughman churl
Has spied and ravished from the nest unfledged:
Nightlong she weeps, and perched upon a bough
Renews her melancholy song, and fills

The country near and far with doleful plaints.
No thoughts of love, no bridal rites have power
To move his soul. Over the northern ice,
By snowy Tanais, and through those plains
Bound fast for ever by Rhipaean frosts,
Alone he roams, lamenting still his lost
Eurydice, and Pluto's cancelled boon.
Angered by such devotion, as though scorned,   520
The Thracian matrons, mid their sacred revels
And orgies of nocturnal Bacchus, rent
The youth piecemeal, and strewed him o'er the land.
Even then, while Oeagrian Hebrus swept
And rolled along in mid-current that head
Torn from its marble neck, *Eurydice!*
The voice still cried; *Ah, poor Eurydice!*
Wailed the cold mouth with fleeting breath; *Eurydice!*
From bank to bank re-echoed the wide stream.'
Thus Proteus; then at a bound plunged himself down
Into the deep sea; and beneath his plunge
He churned the water into foaming eddies.

   Not so Cyrene. To the wildered youth   530
Straightway she spoke: 'My son, now from your soul
You may cast off its burden of sad care.
This then was the whole cause of that disease;
Hence it is that the Nymphs, with whom Eurydice
Was wont to dance in the deep wood, have sent
This miserable destruction on your bees.
A suppliant, you must offer gifts and pray
For reconcilement, worshipping those kindly
Deities of the glens; for at your prayer
They will grant pardon and remit their wrath.
But first the ritual of your supplication
In each detail will I expound. Choose out
Four noble bulls of peerless form, that now
Are grazing with your herds upon the heights
Of green Lycaeus, and as many heifers
Whose necks ne'er felt the yoke. For these set up   540

Four altars by the tall shrines of the Nymphs.
Drain from their throats the sacred blood, but leave
Their bodies lying in the shady grove.
Afterwards, when the ninth dawn shall display
Her rising beams, to Orpheus must you bring
Funeral offerings of Lethaean poppies;
Then, after sacrificing a black ewe,
Visit the grove once more. Eurydice,
Thus appeased, with a slain calf you must worship.'
   Not a moment's tarrying; straightway he performs
His mother's bidding. To the shrines he comes;
He builds the appointed altars, and leads thither
Four noble bulls of peerless form, as many   550
Heifers whose necks have never felt the yoke.
Then, soon as the ninth dawn has ushered in
Her rising beams, funeral gifts he brings
To Orpheus, and once more visits the grove.
And now a sudden marvellous prodigy
Their eyes behold: in the dissolving flesh
Of the oxen bees are buzzing, and from their bellies
Everywhere swarming through the ruptured sides,
Then trailing in vast clouds, till now at last
To a tree's top they stream together, and there
Hang in a cluster from a bending branch.
   Thus did I sing the husbandry of fields,
Of cattle, and of trees, while mighty Caesar   560
By deep Euphrates hurled war's thunderbolts,
A victor, giving laws to willing nations,
And set his foot upon the road to Heaven.
In those days I, Virgil, nursed in the lap
Of sweet Parthenope,[1] went my flowery way
Wooing the studies of inglorious peace;
I who once, dallying with the sportive lays
Of shepherds, in youth's boldness sang of thee,
Tityrus, under the spreading beech tree's shade.

[1] Naples.